Life
LESSONS

LIFE
LESSONS

Two Experts on Death & Dying Teach Us
About the Mysteries of Life & Living

ELISABETH KÜBLER-ROSS, M.D.
& DAVID KESSLER

**SIMON &
SCHUSTER**

London · New York · Sydney · Toronto · New Delhi

A CBS COMPANY

First published in the US by Simon & Schuster Inc., 2000
First published in Great Britain by Simon & Schuster UK Ltd, 2001
This trade paperback edition published by Simon & Schuster UK Ltd, 2014
A CBS COMPANY

1 3 5 7 9 10 8 6 4 2

Simon & Schuster UK Ltd
1st Floor
222 Gray's Inn Road
London WC1X 8HB

www.simonandschuster.co.uk

Simon & Schuster Australia, Sydney
Simon & Schuster India, New Delhi

A CIP catalogue record for this book
is available from the British Library

ISBN: 978-1-47113-986-4
Ebook ISBN: 978-1-47113-987-1

Designed by Erich Hobbing
Printed and bound by CPI (UK) Ltd, Croydon, CR0 4YY

ACKNOWLEDGMENTS

To Ana, who keeps my household going and allows me to stay home instead of going to a nursing home. And my children, Barbara and Kenneth, for keeping me going.

—ELISABETH

First and foremost, my deep thanks to Elisabeth for the privilege of cowriting this book with you. Your wisdom, authenticity, and friendship have made it the experience of a lifetime. Thanks to Al Lowman at Authors and Artists for believing in the importance of this work. Your guidance, support, and friendship are true gifts in my life.

My gratitude to Caroline Sutton at Simon & Schuster for her insight, care, and masterful editing. Thanks also to Elaine Chaisson, Ph.D., B. G. Dilworth, Barry Fox, Linda Hewitt, Christopher Landon, Marianne Williamson, Charlotte Patton, Berry Perkins, Teri Ritter, R.N., Jaye Taylor, James Thommes, M.D., and Steve Uribe, M.F.T., who have each in their special ways made a contribution to this book.

—DAVID

CONTENTS

PREFACE TO
THE ANNIVERSARY EDITION

When Scribner told me that they were releasing an anniversary edition of *Life Lessons,* I was struck by how proud this would have made my coauthor, Elisabeth Kübler-Ross, who died in the summer of 2004.

I am thrilled that this book is as relevant or more relevant now than it was at the time of its first release. That's because it's about how to live in every moment with the knowledge that we don't have forever, so we need to make the most of each and every day.

Life Lessons asks us, "Is this really how I want to live my life?" Since the book came out years ago, it seems that life has sped up. We do more, we move faster, we have more to juggle, our to-do lists are longer, and it feels like we just can't quite catch up with ourselves. And we are getting older. The baby boomers have passed midlife while the next generation is right in the middle of it. As we age, we ask ourselves, "If I keep doing what I'm currently doing, won't I just get more of the same? Is that what I want, or do I want my life to have a higher quality, to be more loving and more peaceful?"

There may be countless books on how to live a better life, but this book is special because both Elisabeth and I shared a unique perspective that came from sitting at the bedsides of the dying. We listened and we learned how life looks when a person is at that edge. We discovered what had meaning, what people regretted, and what they would have done differently.

I have always considered the private time with family members and their dying loved ones to be the ultimate privilege because in those last moments as we teeter on the edge of life, all pretense is stripped away. It is then that people often reveal their deepest truths about what matters most to them. And those last truths are the key to living a happy life.

We all are seeking the elusive answers about how to live, and that's why among all the books I have written, *Life Lessons* still generates a great deal of interest. Now, years later, I am happy to say that it has become a favorite of book clubs around the world, as well as a whole new generation of readers. Many people love the relationship chapter. They tell me that they had never thought about love in the way it shows up in the book. Others say that their attitudes toward money have been greatly improved by the chapter on finances. Many say the chapter on authenticity helped them find their true natures and that this book challenged them and helped them grow on a variety of levels.

That was the vision Elisabeth and I originally shared for *Life Lessons*. However, the truth is that at the time we wrote it, I was not aware of how much I needed to learn the lessons myself.

Each of us has had to come face-to-face with our personal blind spots at times, and for me, one of those moments occurred when I was finishing the chapter on play and how it is so important in our lives. I had a weekend to edit what Elisabeth and I had written about playing when my nephew, Jeffrey, called to invite me to dinner and a movie. "I'd love to," I told him, "but I don't have time."

"How about just dinner?" he asked, but I didn't have time for that either.

"Just a quick cup of coffee?"

I explained how crunched for time I was and that editing the chapter was my priority. While we were winding down the conversation, he asked, "So which chapter are you working on?"

"Making time to play," I said with a straight face. "It's about the importance of having a balanced life and the ability to create play time instead of being so work-oriented."

"Well," Jeffrey told me, "I see you really need to write this chapter. Hope you get it."

"Me, too," I said, still unaware that he was pointing something out to me.

The next time I saw Jeffrey, he let me in on the joke, which had gone right over my head. Luckily, I did eventually get the lesson. I am so grateful that I made my relationship with Jeffrey a priority, since he unexpectedly died in 2011.

I understand now that this book is a journey toward happiness and each time I reread it, I discover a new nugget. Then I think back to when we wrote it and I remember how much the writing inspired Elisabeth as well as me.

Elisabeth and I laughed and cried while we wrote this book. I believe if a book doesn't impact the writers, it won't impact anyone else either. We were impacted! We knew this was information that should be passed on. I am so proud to have had this experience with her. She had a passion for life. She knew how precious life was and how to make the most of it.

Now it is our turn to make the most out of life. I am honored that this book continues to inspire so many people in so many ways. My deepest hope is that it does the same for you.

DAVID KESSLER, 2014

A MESSAGE FROM ELISABETH

We all have lessons to learn during this time called life; this is especially apparent when working with the dying. The dying learn a great deal at the end of life, usually when it is too late to apply. After moving to the Arizona desert in 1995, I had a stroke on Mother's Day that left me paralyzed. I spent the next few years at death's door. Sometimes I thought death would come within a few weeks. Many times, I was disappointed that it did not come, for I was ready. But I have not died because I am still learning the lessons of life, my final lessons. These lessons are the ultimate truths about our lives; they are the secrets to life itself. I wanted to write one more book, not on death and dying but on life and living.

Each of us has a Gandhi and a Hitler in us. I mean this symbolically. The Gandhi refers to the best in us, the most compassionate in us, while the Hitler to the worst in us, our negatives and smallness. Our lessons in life involve working on our smallness, getting rid of our negativity and finding the best in ourselves and each other. These lessons are the windstorms of life, they make us who we are. We are here to heal one another and ourselves. Not healing as in physical recovery, but a much deeper healing. The healing of our spirits, our souls.

When we talk about learning our lessons, we're talking about getting rid of unfinished business. Unfinished business isn't about death. It's about life. It addresses our most important issues, such as "Yes, I made a nice living but did I ever take time out to really live?" Many people have existed, yet never really lived. And they expended tremendous amounts of energy keeping a lid on their unfinished business.

Since unfinished business is the biggest problem in life, it's also the primary issue we address as we face death. Most of us pass on with a great deal of unfinished business; many of us have at least some. There are so many lessons to learn in life, it's impossible to master them all in one lifetime. But the more lessons we learn the more business we finish, and the more fully we live, really live life. And no matter when we die, we can say, "God, I have lived!"

A MESSAGE FROM DAVID

I have spent a great deal of time with people at the edge of life. This work has been enriching and life expanding. I can trace much of my growth, psychologically, emotionally, and spiritually, to my work with the dying. While I am deeply grateful to those I have worked with and who have taught me so much, my lessons did not begin with them. Instead, they began many years ago with my own mother's death and continue to the present as I lose people I love.

During the past few years I have been preparing to say good-bye to a teacher, mentor, and dear, dear friend, Elisabeth. I have spent a great deal of time with her, being taught final lessons. Having taught me so much about my work with the dying, she was now facing death in her own life. She shared how she was feeling—angry a lot of the time—and her views on life. She was completing her last book, *The Wheel of Life,* and I was writing my first, *The Needs of the Dying.* Even during this challenging time of her life she was profoundly helpful to me, dispensing advice on publishing, my patients, and life itself.

Many times, it was enormously hard for me to leave her house. We would say our good-byes, both believing that this would be the last time we would see each other. I would walk away in tears. It is so hard to lose someone who has meant so much, yet she said she was ready. But Elisabeth did not die; she slowly got better. She was not finished with life and it was clearly not finished with her.

In days long gone, the community would have gathering places where children and adults listened as the older men and women told stories of life, of life's challenges and the lessons that can be drawn from the edge of life. People knew that sometimes our greatest lessons lie in our greatest pain. And they knew that it was important to the dying, as well as to the living, that these lessons be passed on. That is what I hope to do, pass on some of the lessons I have learned. Doing so ensures that the best parts of those who have died will live on.

We find many things on this long, sometimes strange journey we see as life, but we mostly find ourselves. Who we really are, what matters most to us. We learn from peaks and valleys what love and relationships really are. We find the courage to push through our anger, tears, and fears. In the mystery of all this, we have been given all we need to make life work—to find happiness. Not perfect lives, not storybook tales, but authentic lives that can make our hearts swell with meaning.

I had the privilege of spending time with Mother Teresa a few months before she died. She told me that her most important work was with the dying, because she considered life so precious. "A life is an achievement," she said, "and dying, the end of that achievement." Not only do most of us not see death as an achievement, we don't see our lives as achievements—and yet, they are.

The dying have always been teachers of great lessons, for it's when we are pushed to the edge of life that we see life most clearly. In sharing their lessons, the dying teach us much about the preciousness of life itself. In them we discover the hero, that part that *transcends all* we have been through and *delivers us to all* we are capable of *doing and being*. To not just be alive, but to *feel* alive.

A NOTE TO THE READER

This book is the result of a close collaboration between Elisabeth Kübler-Ross and David Kessler. The case histories and personal experiences are taken from their lectures, workshops, and discussions with patients and families. Sometimes they involve David, sometimes Elisabeth, and sometimes both. For clarity, we use the "we" voice of Elisabeth and David throughout, except in case histories and personal experiences, where Elisabeth's are preceded by her initials, EKR, or David's by his, DK.

LIFE
LESSONS

CHAPTER ONE

The Lesson
of Authenticity

Stephanie, a woman in her early forties, shared this story at a lecture:

"One Friday afternoon several years ago, I was on my way from Los Angeles to Palm Springs. This is not the best time to take on the Los Angeles freeway traffic, but I was anxious to get to the desert to spend a relaxing weekend with friends.

"At the outskirts of Los Angeles, the cars in front of me came to a standstill. As I came to a stop behind a long line of cars, I glanced in my rearview mirror to discover that the car behind me was not stopping. In fact, it was hurling toward me with tremendous speed. I realized that the driver was not paying attention, that I was going to be hit, and hit hard. I knew that given his speed and the fact that I was nose-to-rear with the car stopped in front of me, I was in great danger. I realized, in that moment, that I might die.

"I looked down at my hands clenched on the steering wheel. I hadn't consciously tightened them; this was my natural state, and this is how I lived life. I decided that I did not want to live that way, nor did I want to die that way. I closed my eyes, took a breath, and dropped my hands to my side. I let go. I surrendered to life, and to death. Then I was hit with enormous force.

"When the movement and noise stopped, I opened my eyes. I was fine. The car in front of me was wrecked, the car behind me was demolished. My car was compacted like an accordion.

"The police told me I was lucky I had relaxed, for muscle tension increases the likelihood of severe injury. I walked away feeling that I had been given a gift. The gift wasn't just that I had survived unhurt, it was greater than that. I saw how I had been living life and was given the opportunity to change. I had held life with a clenched fist, but now I realized that I could hold it in my open hand, as if it were a feather resting on my palm. I realized that if I could relax enough to release my fear in the face of death, I could now truly enjoy life. In that moment, I felt more connected to myself than I ever had before."

Like many others at the edge of life, Stephanie learned a lesson—not about death, but about life and living.

Deep inside all of us, we know there is someone we were meant to be. And we can feel when we're becoming that person. The reverse is also true. We know when something's off and we're not the person we were meant to be.

Consciously or not, we are all on a quest for answers, trying to learn the lessons of life. We grapple with fear and guilt. We search for meaning, love, and power. We try to understand fear, loss, and time. We seek to discover who we are and how we can become truly happy. Sometimes we look for these things in the faces of our loved ones, in religion, God, or other places where they reside. Too often, however, we search for them in money, status, the "perfect" job, or other places, only to find that these things lack the meaning we had hoped to find and even bring us heartaches. Following these false trails without a deeper understanding of their meaning, we are inevitably left feeling empty, believing that there is little or no meaning to life, that love and happiness are simply illusions.

Some people find meaning through study, enlightenment, or creativity. Others discover it while looking at unhappiness, or even death, directly in the eye. Perhaps they were told by their doctors they had cancer or had only six months to live. Maybe they watched loved ones battle for life or were threatened by earthquakes or other disasters.

They were at the edge. They were also on the brink of a new life. Looking right into the "eye of the monster," facing death directly, completely and fully, they surrendered to it—and their view of life was forever changed as they learned a lesson of life. These people had to decide, in the darkness of despair, what they wanted to do with the rest of their life. Not all of these lessons are enjoyable to learn, but everyone finds that they enrich the texture of life. So why wait until the end of life to learn the lessons that could be learned now?

What are these lessons life asks us to master? In working with the dying and the living, it becomes clear that most of us are challenged by the same lessons: the lesson of fear, the lesson of guilt, the lesson of anger, the lesson of forgiveness, the lesson of surrender, the lesson of time, the lesson of patience, the lesson of love, the lesson of relationships, the lesson of play, the lesson of loss, the lesson of power, the lesson of authenticity, and the lesson of happiness.

Learning lessons is a little like reaching maturity. You're not suddenly more happy, wealthy, or powerful, but you understand the world around you better, and you're at peace with yourself. Learning life's lessons is not about making your life perfect, but about seeing life as it was meant to be. As one man shared, "I now delight in the imperfections of life."

We're put here on earth to learn our own lessons. No one can tell you what your lessons are; it is part of your personal journey to discover them. On these journeys we may be given a lot, or just a little bit, of the things we must grapple with, but never more than we can handle. Someone who needs to learn about love may be married many times, or never at all. One who must wrestle with the lesson of money may be given none at all, or too much to count.

We will look at life and living in this book, discovering how life is seen from its outer edge. We will learn that we are not alone, seeing instead how we are all connected, how love grows, how relationships enrich us. Hopefully, we will correct the perception that we are weak, realizing that not only do we have power, we have all the power of the universe within ourselves. We will learn the truth about our illusions, about happiness and the grandness of who we really are. We will learn how we have been given everything we need to make our lives work beautifully.

In facing loss, the people we have worked with realized that love is all that matters. Love is really the only thing we can possess, keep with us, and take with us. They've stopped looking for happiness "out there." Instead, they've learned how to find richness and meaning in those things they already have and are, to dig deeper into the possibilities that are already there. In short, they've broken down the walls that "protected" them from life's fullness. They no longer live for tomorrow, waiting for the exciting news about the job or the family, for the raise or the vacation. Instead, they have found the richness of every *today,* for they have learned to listen to their heart.

Life hands us lessons, universal truths teaching us the basics about love, fear, time, power, loss, happiness, relationships, and authenticity. We are not unhappy today because of the complexities of life. We are unhappy because we miss its underlying simplicities. The true challenge is to find the pure meaning in these lessons. Many of us think we were taught about love. Yet we do not find love fulfilling, because it's not love. It is a shadow darkened by fear, insecurities, and expectations. We walk the earth together yet feel alone, helpless, and ashamed.

When we face the worst that can happen in any situation, we grow. When circumstances are at their worst, we can find our best. When we find the true meaning of these lessons, we also find happy, meaningful lives. Not perfect, but authentic. We can live life profoundly.

Perhaps this is the first and least obvious question: Who is it that is learning these lessons? *Who am I?*

We ask ourselves this question over and over again during our lives. We know for sure that between birth and death there is an experience that we call life. But am I the experience or the experiencer? Am I this body? Am I my faults? Am I this disease? Am I a mother, banker, clerk, or sports fan? Am I a product of my upbringing? Can I change—and still be me—or am I cast in stone?

You are none of those things. You undoubtedly have faults, but they are not you. You may have a disease, but you are not your diagnosis. You may be rich, but you are not your credit rating. You are not your résumé, your neighborhood, your grades, your mistakes, your body, your roles or titles. All these things are not you because they are changeable. There is a part of you that is indefinable and changeless, that does not get lost or change with age, disease, or circumstances.

There is an authenticity you were born with, have lived with, and will die with. You are simply, *wonder-fully,* you.

Watching those who battle illness makes it clear that to see who we are we must shed everything that is not authentically us. When we see the dying, we no longer see those faults, mistakes, or diseases that we focused on before. Now we see only *them,* because at the end of life they become more genuine, more honest, more themselves—just like children and infants.

Are we only able to see who we actually are at life's beginnings and endings? Do only extreme circumstances reveal ordinary truths? Are we otherwise blind to our genuine selves? This is the key lesson of life: to find our authentic selves, and to see the authenticity in others.

The great Renaissance artist Michelangelo was once asked how he created sculptures such as the *Pietà*s or *David.* He explained that he simply imagined the statue *already inside* the block of rough marble, then chipped away the excess to reveal what had always been there. The marvelous statue, already created and eternally present, was waiting to be revealed. So is the great person already inside of you ready to be revealed. *Everyone* carries the seeds of greatness. "Great" people don't have something that everyone else doesn't; they've simply removed a lot of the things that stand in the way of their best selves.

Unfortunately, our inherent gifts are often hidden by layers of masks and roles we've assumed. The roles—such as parent, worker, pillar of community, cynic, coach, outsider, cheerleader, nice guy, rebel, or loving child caring for ailing parent—can become "rocks" burying our true selves.

Sometimes roles are thrust upon us: "I expect you to study hard and grow up to be a doctor." "Be ladylike." "Here at the firm, you must be efficient and diligent if you expect to advance."

Sometimes we eagerly assume roles because they are, or seem to be, useful, uplifting, or lucrative: "Mom always did it this way, so that's probably a good idea." "All Scout leaders are noble and sacrificing, so I will be noble and sacrificing." "I don't have any friends at school, the popular kids are surfers, so I'll be a surfer."

Sometimes we consciously or unwittingly adopt new roles as circumstances change and are hurt by the result. For instance, a couple may say, "It was so wonderful before we got married. Once we were married, something went wrong." When the couple was together before, they were just being. The moment they got married they took on the roles that had been taught to them, trying to "be a husband" and "be a wife." On some subconscious level they "knew" what a husband or wife should be like and tried to act accordingly instead of being themselves and discovering what kind of spouses they wanted to be. Or, as one man explained, "I was such a great uncle, now I feel so disappointed in the father I've become." As an uncle, he interacted with children from his heart. When he became a father, he felt he had a specific role to assume, but that role got in the way of his being who he is, authentically himself.

❖ EKR

It's not always easy to find out who you authentically are. As many of you know, I was born one of a set of triplets. In those days, triplets were dressed alike, given the same toys, enrolled in all the same activities, and so on. People even responded to you not as individuals, but as a set. No matter how good we three were in school, I quickly learned that whether I tried or not, we would always get C's. One of us may have earned A's and another F's, but the teachers always confused us, so it was safer to give all of us C's. Sometimes when I would sit in my father's lap, I knew he did not know which one I was. Can you imagine what this does to your identity? Now we know how important it is to recognize the individual, to recognize how different each of us is. These days, when multiple births have become routine, parents have learned not to dress and treat their kids alike.

Being a triplet began my search for authenticity. I have always tried to be myself, even when being myself may have not been the most popular choice. I don't believe in being a phony-baloney for any reason.

Throughout my life, as I've learned to be my real self, I've developed a knack for recognizing others who are authentically themselves. I call it sniffing someone out. You don't smell with your nose, you smell with all your senses if someone is real or not. I've learned to sniff people when I meet them and if they smell real, I give them a signal to come close. If not, I give them a signal to go away. In working with the dying you develop a keen sense of smell for authenticity.

At times in my life the inauthenticity was not obvious; other times it was very much so. For example, people often want to look like the "nice person" by driving me to my lectures and pushing me in my wheelchair to the stage. But then, once that's happened, I often have trouble finding a way home. I realized in those situations that I was just being used to inflate their egos. If they were really nice people and not just assuming the role, they would also want to make sure I got home okay.

❖ ❖ ❖

Most of us play many roles throughout our lifetimes. We have learned how to shift roles, but we don't often know how to look behind them. The roles we assume—spouse, parent, boss, nice guy, rebel, etc.—are not necessarily bad and can provide useful models to follow in unfamiliar situations. Our task is to find those parts that work for us, and those that don't. It is like peeling the layers of an onion, and just like peeling an onion, it's a task that can bring on a few tears.

It may be painful, for example, to acknowledge the negativity in ourselves and find ways to externalize it. Each of us contains the potential to be anything from Gandhi to Hitler. Most of us do not like the idea that we contain a Hitler; we don't want to hear it. But we all have a negative side, or a potential for negativity: denying it is the most dangerous thing we can do. It's cause for concern when some people completely deny the potentially dark side of themselves, insisting that they are not capable of strongly negative thoughts or actions. To admit we have the capacity for negativity is essential. After admitting it, we can work on and release it. And as we learn our lessons, we often strip away layers of roles to find things we're not happy about. It doesn't mean that who we are, that our essence, is bad. It means we had a facade we didn't recognize. If you discover you're not a supernice person, it's time to shed that image and be who you are, because being an extraordinarily nice person every moment of your life is being a phony-baloney. Many times the pendulum has to swing all the way to the other side (you become a grump) before it can come back to the middle point where you discover who you really are— someone who is nice out of compassion rather than someone who is giving to get.

Even more challenging is to let go of defense mechanisms

that helped us survive in childhood, because once these tools are no longer needed they can turn against us. A woman learned when she was a child to isolate herself from her alcoholic father: she knew that it was best to leave the situation and leave the room when it became overwhelming. This was the only tool a six-year-old girl could come up with when her father was drunk and yelling. It helped her survive a difficult childhood, but now that she herself is a mother, such withdrawal is harmful to her children. Tools that no longer work must be released. We must thank them and let them go. And sometimes people have to grieve for that part of them that will never be. This mother had to grieve for the normal childhood she was never granted.

Sometimes we get a lot out of these roles, but we often realize with maturity that they have a cost. At a certain point the cost becomes too much to bear. Many people are well into middle age before realizing that they have been the "forever caretaker and peacemaker" in their family. When they understand this, they'll say that they certainly are nice, but it got pushed way out of proportion in their family. Without seeing what was happening, they took on the responsibility of making sure their parents and siblings were always happy, they solved all the fights, loaned everyone money, helped them get jobs. At some point, you may realize that the burdensome role is not you, so you drop it. You're still a nice person, but you no longer feel obligated to make sure everyone else is happy.

The reality of the world is that some relationships don't work out; there are supposed to be disagreements and disappointments. If you feel responsible for fixing every problem, you will pay a high price because that's an impossible task.

How will you respond to the new you?

- You might realize that the role was a chore: "It's great now that I don't feel responsible for everyone's happiness."
- You might realize that you were deceiving others: "I was manipulating everyone, trying to get them to like me more by being nice."
- You might realize that you are lovable just as you authentically are.
- You might find that your actions came out of fear: fear of not being good, fear of not going to heaven, fear of not being liked.
- You might realize that you were using the role to win trophies: "I always thought I'd become that person everyone loved and admired, but I'm just human like everyone else."
- You might realize that it's safe for other people to have problems, that they are on their path to finding out who they are.
- You might realize that you make them weak, so that you feel stronger.
- You might realize that by focusing on what's "broken" in them, you avoid your own issues.

Most of us have not committed criminal acts, but we do have to work through the darker parts of our personalities. Black and white are apparent; it's those gray parts that we often hide and deny: the "nice" guy, the isolator, the victim, and the martyr. These are the gray parts of our shadow self. We can't work on the deep negativity if we can't admit that we have negative sides. If we acknowledge all of our feelings, we can become our *whole selves*.

You might mourn for the loss of these roles, but you'll know you're better off because you're more genuinely you.

Who you are is eternal; it never has and never will change.

Who we are is much more than our circumstances, whether they be great or small, though we tend to define ourselves by our circumstances. If it is a great day—if the weather's good, the stock market is up, the car is clean and shiny, the kids get good report cards, the dinner-and-show goes well—we feel as if we are great people. If not, we feel as if we're worthless. We move with the tide of events, some controllable, others not. But who we are is much more unchanging than that. It is not defined by this world or our roles. These are all illusions, myths that do not serve us well. Underneath all our circumstances, all our situations, is a great person. We discover our true identities and greatness by letting go of all the illusions of identity to discover our true selves.

We often look to others to define us. If others are in a bad mood, we are brought down. If others see us as being wrong, we become defensive. But who we are is beyond attack and defense. We are whole, complete, and of worth just as we are, whether we are rich or poor, old or young, receiving an Olympic gold medal, or beginning or ending a relationship. Whether at the beginning or the end of life, at the height of fame or in the depths of despair, we are always the people behind our circumstances. You are what you are, not your disease, not what you do. Life is about being, not doing.

✤DK

I asked a woman who was dying, "Who are you now?" She said, "In all the roles I had, I felt so common, I felt like I had lived a life so many other people could have lived. What made my life different from anyone else's?

"What I've realized through my illness was so eye-opening for me: I'm truly a unique person. No one else has ever seen or experienced the world in quite the way I have. And no one else ever will. Since the beginning of time, until the end of time, there will never be another me."

This is as true for you as it was for her. No one has ever experienced the world in quite the way you have, with your particular history and the events that happened to you. Who you are is unique beyond comprehension. But not until we discover who we truly are can we begin to celebrate our uniqueness.

Many people have serious breakdowns when they realize they don't know who they are; trying to get to know themselves for the first time is a daunting task. They realize they don't know how to react to themselves as themselves, as opposed to who they think they should be.

When people are hit with life-challenging diagnoses, they may, for the first time, have to figure out who they are. Asking ourselves "Who is dying?" usually leads to the answer that a part of ourselves doesn't die, but continues, has always been. When the day comes that we're ill and can no longer be the banker, traveler, doctor, or coach, we have to ask ourselves an important question: "If I'm not those things, then who am I?" If you're no longer the nice guy at the office, the selfish uncle, the helpful neighbor, who are you?

Discovering and being authentic to ourselves, finding out what we want to do and do not want to do—we do this by being committed to our own experiences. We must do everything because it brings us joy and peace, from the job we have to the clothes we wear. If we do something to make ourselves worthy in the eyes of others, we are not seeing the worth in ourselves. It's amazing how much more we live by what we *should* do than by what we *want* to do.

Once in a while, give in to an urge you would usually suppress, try doing something "odd" or new. You may learn something about who you are. Or ask yourself what you would do if no one was looking. If you could do anything you wanted, without consequences, what would it be? Your answer to that question reveals a lot about who you are, or at least what is in your way. Your answer may point to a negative belief about yourself, or a lesson to work on before you can discover your essence.

If you say you would steal, you probably fear that you do not have enough.

If you say you would lie, you probably do not feel safe telling the truth.

If you say you would love someone whom you are not loving now, you may fear love.

♣DK

I always rushed around on vacations, getting up early in the morning, seeing and doing as many things as possible during the day, returning to my hotel late at night exhausted. Finally realizing that I never had any fun on my vacations, that they were always stressful, I asked myself what I would do if nobody was looking. The answer was that I'd sleep late, see a few sites at a leisurely pace, and sit on the veranda or beach for at least an hour a day reading a good book or just doing nothing. The role of "enthusiastic vacationer seeing absolutely everything" wasn't me. I did it because I thought

I should, but I was much happier when I realized that I had more fun, and learned more, when I mixed sight-seeing with relaxing.

What would you do if your parents, society, boss, teacher, weren't around? How would you define yourself? Who is under all that stuff? That's the real you.

❖ ❖ ❖

At age sixty, Tim, the father of three daughters, had a heart attack. He had been a good father to the now grown trio, whom he had raised on his own. After the heart attack he began to examine his life. "I realized it was not only my arteries that had hardened," he explained. "I had hardened. It happened years ago when my wife died. I needed to be strong. I wanted the girls to grow up strong, too. So I was tough on them. Now that task is over. I'm sixty, my life will soon be over. I don't want to be tough anymore. I want the girls to know they have a father who loves them very much."

In his hospital room he told his daughters of his love. They had always known about it, but this softening brought tears to everyone's eyes. He no longer felt he had to be the father he should be, and may have had to have been, back then. Instead, he could be the person he was inside.

We're not all geniuses like Einstein or great athletes like Michael Jordan, but "chipping away the excess" will allow us all to be brilliant in one way or another, depending on our own gifts.

Who you are is the purest of love, the grandest kind of perfection. You are here to heal yourself and to remember who you have always been. It is your guiding light in the darkness.

Trying to find out who you are will lead you to the work you need to do, the lessons you need to learn. When our inner and outer beings are one, we no longer need to hide, fear, or protect ourselves. We see who we are as something that transcends our circumstances.

❖D K

Late one evening, I was speaking to a man in a hospice. He was suffering from ALS (Lou Gehrig's disease). "What's the hardest part of this experience for you," I asked. "The hospitalization? The disease?"

"No," he replied. "The hardest part is that everyone sees me in the past tense. Something that once was. No matter what's going on with my body, I will still be a whole person. There is a part of me that is not definable and doesn't change, that I will not lose and does not disappear with age or disease. There is a part of myself that I cling to. That is who I am and that is who I will always be."

The man discovered that the essence of who he was went way beyond what was going on with his body, how much money he had made, or how many children he had fathered. After we strip away these roles, *we* are what's left. There is within each of us a potential for goodness beyond our imagining, for giving without seeking reward, for listening without judging, for loving unconditionally. That potential is our goal. We can approach it in large ways and small ways every minute of the day, if we try. Many people, touched by illness and wishing to touch others, have worked through their own growth. They move toward a completion of their unfinished business and are now in a position to light candles for others.

Who we are means honoring the integrity of our human selves. That sometimes includes those dark parts of our beings that we often try to hide. We think sometimes we're only drawn to the good, but we're actually drawn to the authentic. We like people who are real more than those who hide their true selves under layers of artificial niceties.

❖EKR

Years ago, at the University of Chicago Medical School, I was fortunate to be selected as "favorite professor." This was one of the biggest honors we professors could receive; we all wanted to be recognized by our students. The day it was announced that I had won, everyone acted nicely toward me, as they usually did. But no one said anything to me about the award. I sensed something behind their smiles, something they weren't saying. Toward the end of that day a gorgeous flower arrangement arrived at my office from one of my colleagues, a child psychiatrist. The card read, "Jealous as hell, congratulations anyway." From that moment on I knew I could trust that man. I loved him for being so real, so authentic. I would always feel that I knew where he stood and feel safe around him, because he showed his true self.

The grandest kind of perfection of who we are includes being honest about our dark sides, our imperfections. We find comfort when we know who someone else is. And it is just as important that we learn the truth about ourselves, the truth about who we are.

A man shared the story of his grandmother, who, in her late seventies, was very ill. "I was having so much trouble letting her go," he explained. "I finally got up the courage to say to her, 'Nana, I don't think I can let you go.' I know that sounds selfish, but it's what I felt.

"'My dear one,' she replied, 'I am complete, my life has been full and whole. I know you must see me not being full of much life anymore, but I assure you I have brought much life to my journey. We are like a pie: we give a piece to our parents, we give a piece to our loves, we give a piece to our children, and we give a piece to our careers. At the end of life, some people have not saved a piece for themselves—and don't even know what kind of pie they were. I know what kind of pie I am; this is something we each find for ourselves. I can leave this life knowing who I am.'

"When I heard those words, 'I now know who I am,' I could let her go. That did it for me. It sounded so complete. I told her when it was my time to die, I hoped I would be like her and know who I am. She leaned forward, as if to tell me a secret, and said, 'You don't have to wait until you are dying to find out what kind of pie you are.'"

CHAPTER TWO

THE LESSON OF LOVE

Love, that thing we have great difficulty even describing, is the only truly real and lasting experience of life. It is the opposite of fear, the essence of relationships, the core of creativity, the grace of power, an intricate part of who we are. It is the source of happiness, the energy that connects us and that lives within us.

Love has nothing to do with knowledge, education, or power; it is beyond behavior. It is also the only gift in life that is not lost. Ultimately, it is the only thing we can really give. In a world of illusions, a world of dreams and emptiness, love is the source of truth.

For all its power and grandness, however, it is elusive. Some spend their lives searching for love. We are afraid we will never have it, that if we find it, we will lose it or take it for granted, fearing it will not last.

We think we know what love looks like, since we formed pictures of it during childhood. The most common picture is the romantic ideal: when we meet that someone special, we suddenly feel whole, everything is wonderful, and we live happily ever after. Of course, we are brokenhearted when, in real life, we have to fill in the not-so-romantic details, when we find out that most of the love we give and receive is conditional. Even the love for and from our families and friends is based on expectations and conditions. Inevitably, these expectations and conditions are not met, and the details of real life become the thread that creates a nightmare. We find ourselves in loveless friendships and relationships. We wake from our romantic illusions to a world that lacks the love we had hoped for as children. Now taking an adult view of love, we see it all clearly, realistically, and bitterly.

Fortunately, true love *is* possible, we *can* feel the love we had hoped for. It does exist, but not in our approach to love. It does not live in the dream of finding the perfect mate or the best friend. The wholeness we seek lives here, with and within us, now, in reality. We have only to remember.

Most of us want unconditional love, love that exists because of who we are rather than what we do or do not do. If we are lucky, very lucky, we may have experienced a few minutes of it in our lifetimes. Sadly, most of the love we experience in this life is very conditional. We're loved because of what we do for others, how much we earn, how funny we are, how we treat our children or keep our houses, and so on. We find it hard to love people just the way they are. It's almost as if we look for excuses not to love others.

❖EKR

A very proper woman approached me after a lecture. You know what I mean by *proper:* every hair in place, perfectly matched clothes, and so on. "I went to your workshop last year," she said, "On the way home, all I could think of was my eighteen-year-old son. Every night when I come home, he's sitting on the kitchen counter, wearing that horrible, washed-out T-shirt he got from one of his girlfriends. I always fear the neighbors will think that we can't dress our children right if they see him in it.

"He just sits there with his friends." And when she said "friends," her face filled with disgust. "Every night when I come home, I scold him, beginning with that T-shirt. One thing leads to another and . . . Well, that has been our relationship.

"I thought about the life-ending exercise we did in the workshop. I realized that life is a gift, one I will not have forever. And I will not have those I love around me forever, either. I really looked at the what-ifs. What if I died tomorrow, how would I feel about my life? I realized I was okay with my life, even though my relationship with my son was not perfect. Then I thought: What if my son died tomorrow, how would I feel about the life I had given him?

"I realized I would experience enormous loss and deep conflict about our relationship. As I played out the horrible scenario in my mind, I thought about his funeral. I wouldn't want to bury him in a suit; he wasn't a suit kind of kid. I would want to bury him in that damn shirt he loved so much. That is how I would honor him and his life.

"Then I realized, in death I would give him the gift of loving him for who he is and what he likes, but I was unwilling to give him that gift in life.

"I suddenly understood this T-shirt has enormous meaning for him. For whatever reason, it is his favorite. That night, when I came home, I told him it was okay to wear that T-shirt all he wanted. I told him I loved him just the way he was. It felt so good to have let go of the expectations, to stop trying to fix him and just love him as he is. And now that I'm no longer trying to make him perfect, I find that he's very lovable just the way he is."

❖ ❖ ❖

We can only find peace and happiness in love when we release the conditions we place on our love for each other. And we usually place the toughest conditions on those we love the most. We have been taught conditional love well—we have literally been conditioned—which makes this a difficult unlearning process. As human beings, it is not possible to find *complete* unconditional love with one another, but we can find more than just the minutes we usually get in a lifetime.

One of the few places we do find unconditional love is from our children when they are very young. They don't care about our day, our money, or our accomplishments. They just love us. We eventually teach them to put conditions on their love as we reward them for smiling, getting good grades, and being what we want them to be. But we can still learn a lot from the way children love us. If we loved our children just a little more unconditionally, for a little while longer, we might create a very different world to live in.

Conditions on love are weights on our relationships. When we release the conditions, we can find love in many ways we never thought possible.

One of the greatest obstacles to giving unconditional love is our fear that the love may not be returned. We don't realize that the feeling we seek lies in the giving, not in the receiving.

If we measure love received, we will never feel loved. Instead, we will feel shortchanged. Not because we really were, but because the act of measuring is not an act of love. When you feel unloved, it is not because you are not receiving love; it is because you are withholding love.

When you argue with loved ones, you believe you are

upset because of something they did or did not do. You are actually upset because you have closed your heart, you have withdrawn love. And the answer should never be to withhold love until they shape up. What if they don't, what if they never do? Do you never again love your mother, your friend, your brother? But if you love them in spite of what they did, you will see changes, you will see all the power of the universe unleashed. You will see their hearts melt open.

❖D K

A woman shared that she was a flight attendant for TWA. "I was friends with one of the crew members on Flight 800. I had called my friend because she was on my mind. It had been a while since we'd talked and I missed seeing her. I left her a message on her voice mail to call me. A few days went by and I became increasingly irritated that I had not heard back. My husband said just call again or say what you want to say on her answering machine. I knew she was probably busy and was just waiting for some free time to call me back. Even knowing this, I became increasingly angry. I held back my love, I closed my heart to her. The next day her plane crashed. I deeply regret I did not give my love freely. I was playing a game with love."

I told the woman not to be so hard on herself, that her friend knew from their years of friendship that she was loved. The woman needed to forgive herself and realize she was doing the same thing to herself that she had done to her friend with the phone call: she was measuring love by one moment, one action, then closing her heart. We must try to see love in the big picture, not in a detail. A detail such as a single phone call can be a distraction from real love. This woman's story is an example of how the rules, the games, and the measurements interfere with our expression of love for one another. It's a hard lesson to learn.

❖ ❖ ❖

To open our hearts again, we must be open to seeing differently. When we close our hearts, when we are intolerant, it's often because we don't know what is going on with the other person. We don't understand them; we don't know why they don't return our calls or why they're so loud, so we don't love them. We are so ready to talk about our hurt, our pain, and how we have been wronged. The truth is, we betray one another by not freely giving our smiles, our understanding, our love. We withhold the greatest gifts God has given us. Our act of withholding is much more serious than what the other person might or might not have done to us.

Late one night, a ninety-eight-year-old woman spoke about life and love. "I was raised by a mother who distrusted men. They were only to be used for financial security. I became my mother's daughter and never let love into my life. Why should I ask for such trouble? The only man I ever cared for and trusted was my brother. He was everything to me: my big brother, my friend, my protector. He married a wonderful woman. When I was in my late twenties, he became very ill. The doctors were not sure what was wrong. We sat together in the hospital and somehow we both knew he was going to die. I told him I didn't want to live in a world without him. He told me how much life had meant to him and that if this was it, he wouldn't change a thing. Except me. He said, 'I am afraid you are going to miss life, your life, and you'll miss love. Don't miss love. Everyone on this journey we call life should have an experience of love. It ultimately doesn't matter who or when or for how long you love. It just matters that you do. Don't miss it. Don't take the journey without it.'

"I had a life because of my brother's message. I could have continued to not trust men, I could have become less of a woman, less of a person. But I fought past my mistrust and my fears. I have tried to have the life he wanted me to have. He was so right. To have this time, this life, and not love would be to have not experienced life fully."

Many of us learned about "love," or actually, protection, just as this woman did. We learned early not to trust men, women, marriage, parents, in-laws, coworkers, our bosses, and even life itself. We were taught by well-meaning people who felt they were acting in our best interests. They didn't realize they were setting us up to miss out on love.

But in our hearts we know we are destined to live fully, to love fully, and to have great adventures in life. Maybe the feeling is buried deep within, but it's there, waiting to be brought out by an action or an event, perhaps a word from someone else. Our lessons may come from unexpected places, such as children.

❖ EKR

Some years ago, I knew a young boy who was eager to spread love and find life, even though he was at the end of his. He had had cancer for six of his nine years. In the hospital, I took one look at him and knew he was finished fighting. He had just had it. He had accepted the reality of his death. I stopped by to say good-bye the day he was going home. To my surprise, he asked me to go home with him. When I tried to sneak a peak at my watch, he assured me that it would not take long. And so we drove into his driveway and parked.

He told his father to take down his bicycle, which had been hanging in the garage, unused, for three years. His biggest dream was to ride around the block once—he had never been able to do that. He asked his father to put the training wheels on his bicycle. That takes a lot of courage for a little boy to do: it's humiliating to be seen with training wheels when your peers are popping wheelies and performing tricks with their bikes. With tears in his eyes, the father did so.

Then the boy looked at me and said, "Your job is to hold my mom back."

You know how moms are, they want to protect you all the time. She wanted to hold him up all the way around the block, but that would cheat him out of his great victory. His mother understood. She knew that one of the last things she could do for her son was to refrain, out of love, from hovering over him as he undertook his last, great challenge.

We waited as he rode off. It seemed like an eternity. Then he came around the corner, barely able to balance. He was terribly drawn and pale. Nobody thought he could ride a bike. But he rode up to us beaming. Then he had his father take off the training wheels and we carried the bike, and him, upstairs. "When my brother comes home from school, would you send him in?" he asked.

Two weeks later the little brother, a first-grader, told us that his brother had given him the bicycle as a birthday present, since he knew he would not be around for the birthday. With not much time or energy left, this brave boy had lived out his final dreams, riding his bike around the corner and passing it on to his younger sibling.

❖ ❖ ❖

There are dreams of love, life, and adventure in all of us. But we are also sadly filled with reasons why we shouldn't try.

These reasons seem to protect us, but in truth they imprison us. They hold life at a distance. Life will be over sooner than we think. If we have bikes to ride and people to love, now is the time.

❖EKR

As I thought about the lessons of love, I thought about myself and my own life. Naturally, that I'm still alive means I still have lessons to learn. I, like everyone else I've ever worked with, need to learn how to love myself more. I still think of myself as a Swiss hillbilly, so whenever I hear the term *self-love,* I must admit I picture a woman sitting in a corner masturbating. Obviously, because of that, I've never connected with the term very well.

I have felt much love from others in my personal life, as well as through my work over the years. One would assume that if you are loved by so many, you would love yourself. But this is not always true. It's not true for most of us. I've seen it in hundreds of lives and deaths, and now I see it in myself. Love has to come from within, if it is to come at all. And I'm still not there.

❖ ❖ ❖

How can we learn to love ourselves? It's one of our biggest challenges, it's so difficult to do. Most of us never learned to love ourselves as children. We're usually taught that to love ourselves is negative, for love of self is confused with self-absorption and egotism. So, we end up thinking that love consists of meeting Mr. or Ms. Wonderful, or someone who treats us "just right." That has nothing to do with love.

Most of us have never experienced love. We experienced rewards. We learned as children that we would be "loved" if we were polite, got good grades, smiled for Grandma, or washed our hands often enough. We worked our little rears off to be loved, never realizing that this was conditional, thus false, love. How can we possibly love if it takes so much approval from others? We can begin by nurturing our souls, and having compassion for ourselves.

Do you nurture your soul, do you feed it? What activities do you do that make you feel better about yourself, that you're really glad to have done? When we love ourselves, we fill our lives with activities that put smiles on our faces. These are the things that make our hearts and our souls sing. They are not always the "good things" we were taught we should do—they're things we do just for ourselves. Nurturing yourself may be sleeping in late on Saturday instead of getting up and being "productive." And nurturing ourselves is letting the love that is all around us in.

While you're nurturing, have a little compassion for yourself, give yourself a break. So many people call themselves stupid, or say they can't believe they did that, or they're an idiot. If someone else made a mistake, you would say, "Don't worry, it happens to everyone, no big deal." When we make the same mistake, it means we're a worthless failure. Most of us are easier on other people then we are on ourselves. Let's practice being as kind to and forgiving of ourselves as we are to others.

❖ D K

Caroline is a tall, attractive woman in her late forties who learned how to nurture her soul. She has strikingly beautiful black hair and the most genuine smile you will ever see. We got to know each other while working on a project

together, and she stuck me as being one of the happiest people I had ever met. She was in her second year of a wonderful relationship with a smart, kind, witty dentist. They were
making last-minute plans for their wedding, which was just
a few months away, and were exploring the possibility of
adopting a child.

Being out in the world with Caroline was an uplifting
experience. No one is a stranger to her, she's friendly and
close to everyone—the receptionist, the waitress, the person
next to us in a movie line. One night, over dinner, I com-
mented that she was lucky in love. With a little laugh she
said it was not luck, and shared her story.

Six years ago, she had found a lump in her breast. When
the lump was biopsied, the doctor said it looked strange. But
three days would pass before they would know if it was can-
cerous and had spread.

"I thought this was it," she said. "It may end here. All my
unhappiness rose to the surface. Those three days were the
longest of my entire life. I was truly blessed when the results
came back saying that it was not cancer. I decided that even
though I had wonderful news, I was not going to let those
three days wind up meaning nothing, I was not going to live
the same life I had been living.

"The holidays were approaching and I was receiving the
usual invites to parties. The previous Christmas I had been
desperately alone and single. I went to as many parties as
possible, looking for love. I wanted someone to love me, to
give me all the love I was not giving to myself. I'd walk into
a party, quickly scan it for Mr. Right, and if he wasn't there,
I'd rush to the next party. After running from party to party
I'd go home more desperate, more alone than when I had
started the evening.

"I decided I didn't want to do the same thing again this year. There had to be another way. I decided to give myself the experience of loving and being loved. So I made a choice to stop searching. I would go, but if Mr. Right was not there, other people were. Wonderful people I could talk to. I would just talk with them, have fun. I would be open to liking or loving them for who they were, no matter what.

"Now, I know you're thinking that this story ends with me meeting Mr. Right that year. I didn't. But at the end of the evening I didn't feel lonely or desperate, because I had truly talked with people. All the smiles I smiled and all the laughs I laughed that night were real. All the love I felt was genuine. I had a wonderful time. I felt more love from others, and to my surprise, I liked myself a whole lot more.

"I kept doing this throughout the season, not just at parties but at work, at the store, in every possible situation. The more love I gave, the more love I felt. The more love I felt, the easier it became to love myself. I've become closer than ever to my friends, I met some wonderful new people. I became a happier person, someone you would want to meet. I was no longer that desperate, searching person. I experienced love every day."

❖ ❖ ❖

Loving ourselves is receiving the love that is always around us. To love ourselves is to remove all barriers. It's difficult to see the barriers we erect around ourselves, but they're there, and they play into all our relationships.

When we meet God, He will ask, "Did you give and receive love, to yourself and others?" We can learn to love ourselves by letting others love us, and by loving them. God has provided us with unlimited opportunities to love and be loved. They are all around us, they are ours for the taking.

✤ EKR

A thirty-eight-year-old man was diagnosed with prostate cancer. He told me that he had begun to review his life during his treatments, which he was going through alone. As we spoke, his face filled with sadness about this lonely reality. I asked the obvious question: "You seem bright, attractive, and nice, and you seem to want someone here with you. Why is there no wife, no girlfriend?"

"I'm not lucky in love," he replied. "I tried to love them, to make them happy. In my relationships, I would put all my energy into making them happy. But eventually I would disappoint them. When I would begin to see that I couldn't make them happy, I was out of there. It didn't matter, because I could start all over again and there was always somebody else. Now half my life is gone, and it could end much sooner than I expected. I'm beginning to realize that maybe I haven't loved at all. Yet I know I'm not giving a woman what she wants if I can't make her happy. It's easier to just leave."

I asked him a question that he had apparently never thought about: "What if love wasn't making a woman happy? What if, instead, we defined love as being there? We know we really can't make someone else happy all the time. What if your gauge was off, what if simply being there really made them happy, in the long run?"

Life has its up and downs. We can't solve all of our loved ones' problems, but we can usually be there for someone. Isn't that, over the years, the strongest sign of love?

"As you're lying in the hospital, being treated for prostate cancer, it's not likely that a woman—or anyone else—could make you happy," I pointed out to the man. "But wouldn't having someone special here with you, through all of this, mean a lot to you?"

❖ ❖ ❖

❖D K

I often end lectures with the story of a young mother and her daughter, Bonnie, who lived outside of Seattle. It shows the power that even a stranger can have to comfort. One day the mother left six-year-old Bonnie with their next-door neighbor while she went to work. Later in the day, as Bonnie was playing on the neighbor's front lawn, a car came careening around the corner, out of control. It flew up onto the lawn and smashed into the little girl, knocking her into the street.

The police were summoned and came almost instantly. As the first policeman rushed over to the little girl, he saw how severely hurt she was. Unable to do anything to save her, he simply picked the little girl up and held her. He just held her in his arms.

By the time the paramedics arrived, she had stopped breathing. They started life support immediately and rushed her to the hospital. There, the emergency-room team worked on her for over an hour, without success.

One of the nurses, who had been desperately trying to reach Bonnie's mother at work, had to tell the poor woman that the little girl she had kissed sweetly that morning was now gone. The nurse shared this terrible news as gently as possible. Although the hospital offered to send someone to drive the mother in, she insisted on making the long drive herself.

Finally the mother walked into the hospital, stoic until

she saw her little girl lying lifelessly on the table. She completely broke down.

The doctors sat down with her and explained her daughter's injuries and what they had done to try to save her life. This didn't help the mother. The nurses sat down with her and explained how they had done everything possible to save her little girl. The mother remained inconsolable, so grief-stricken that the staff thought they might have to admit this poor mother. Then the devastated mother walked through the emergency room to the pay phone, to call her relatives. Seeing her, the policeman who had been sitting there for almost four hours stood up. He had been the first to arrive on the scene, the one who had held little Bonnie in his arms. He walked up to this mother and told her what had happened, adding, "I just want you to know she was not alone."

The mother was so grateful to hear that in her daughter's last moments on this earth, she was held and loved. The mother finally felt consoled, knowing her daughter had felt love at the end of life, even if it was from a stranger.

❖EKR

Being there is everything in love, in life and in dying. Many years ago, I noticed an interesting phenomenon in a hospital. Many of the dying patients began to feel wonderful; not so much physically, but mentally. This wasn't because of me, but because of the cleaning woman. Every time she walked into the room of one of my dying patients, something would happen. I would have given a million dollars to learn that woman's secret.

One day I saw her in the hallway and said to her rather curtly, "What are you doing with my dying patients?"

"I'm only cleaning the rooms," she replied defensively.

Determined to know how she was making people feel good, I followed her around. But I couldn't figure out what special thing she was doing. After a few weeks of snooping around like this, she grabbed me and dragged me into a room behind the nurses' station. She told me how, some time ago, one of her six children had become very ill one winter. In the middle of the night she took her three-year-old son to the emergency room, where she sat with him on her lap, desperately waiting hours for the physician to come. But no one came, and she watched her little boy die of pneumonia, in her arms. She shared all this pain and agony without hate, without resentment, without anger, without negativity.

"Why are you telling me this?" I asked. "What has this to do with my dying patients?"

"Death is not a stranger to me anymore," she replied. "He is like an old acquaintance. Sometimes when I walk into the rooms of your dying patients, they look so scared. I can't help but walk over to them and touch them. I tell them I've seen death, and when it happens, they will be okay. And I just stay there with them. I may want to run, but I don't. I try to be there for the other person. That is love."

Unschooled in the ways of psychology and medicine, this woman knew one of the greatest secrets in life: love is being there, and caring.

Sometimes, due to circumstances beyond our control, we can't be there physically. But that doesn't mean we're not connected in love.

❖ ❖ ❖

❖DK

Last year I was invited to speak at a conference for doctors and nurses in New Orleans, then teach a class for social workers at Tulane University. It would be a rewarding professional experience, but certainly not a pleasure trip. As the plane landed, I was filled with emotions: this would always be the last place I ever saw my mother alive. After my professional work was completed, I decided to go back to the hospital where my mother had died.

Our local hospital couldn't care for my mother, so she was transferred to this bigger hospital two hours away from our house. I was only thirteen years old. The hospital rules said that visitors had to be at least fourteen years old. So I sat outside the intensive care unit for many hours, waiting for a chance to sneak in and speak to her, to touch her, to simply be with her.

If that wasn't enough, the Howard Johnson's hotel where my father and I stayed, right by the hospital, was suddenly evacuated. My father and I were in the lobby, about to go visit my mother, when all of a sudden a number of police cars screeched to a halt in front of the hotel. Officers dashed inside, shouting for us to evacuate, pushing us out. As we raced out of the building, we heard gunshots. A sniper was standing on the hotel roof, shooting at passersby. My father and I wanted to go right to the hospital to be with my mother, but the authorities wouldn't let us, insisting that we go into the building next to the hospital. Eventually the police gained some control, and we were able to get into the hospital. The sniper was later killed by the police.

At thirteen years old, while needing to see my mother, I was also running out of a hotel while a sniper was shooting at people, and being evacuated from one building to the next. Through all of this, I so desperately wanted to be able to spend a few precious moments with her, to say good-bye.

Now, twenty-six years later, I walked through the small grassy area in front of the hotel, looking at the hospital. I remembered all the excitement and confusion of that day. I stood outside the door to the intensive care unit where my mother had spent the last two weeks of her life, looking through the same window I had peered through twenty-six years earlier, a little boy wishing he could see his mother.

A nurse came around the corner and asked if I wanted to visit someone. As I said "No, thank you," I couldn't help thinking about the irony of the nurses not letting me in years before.

"Are you sure?" she persisted. "You can if you want to."

"No," I answered. "The person I want to see is no longer here, but thank you."

Now, after many years and many lessons, I know that my mother lives on in my heart and mind, and in the words of this page. I also believe she exists elsewhere, in some other way. I can't see her or touch her, but I can feel her. Even in loss and separation, I am clear that I was with my mother in her last days, even though I could not physically be there.

And then there are times when someone else may be there for our loved ones. For these health care professionals—or just kind strangers—simply being there, even when they don't know the name of the person they're there for, is a powerful act of love.

A cleaning lady, a mother, a friend, and a policeman who held a little girl he had never met before—our lessons in love come in all forms, from all kinds of people and situations. It doesn't matter who we are, what we do, how much money we make, whom we know. We can all love and be loved. We can be there, we can open our hearts to the love around us as we give love back, determined not to miss the great gift.

Love is always present in life, in all of our wonderful experiences—and even in our tragedies. Love is what gives our days their deep meaning, it is what we are truly made of. Whatever we may call it—love, God, soul—love is alive and tangible, living within us all. Love is our experience of the divine, of sacred holiness. Love is the richness all around us. It is ours for the taking.

CHAPTER THREE

THE LESSON
OF RELATIONSHIPS

A forty-one-year-old woman remembered an uneventful evening she and her husband had spent several months ago. They ate a simple dinner she had prepared, then watched TV. About 9 P.M. he said his stomach was upset and took an antacid. A few minutes later he said he was going to turn in early. She kissed him good-night, saying she would be in a little later and hoped he would feel better in the morning. An hour and a half later, when she went to bed, her husband was fast asleep.

As soon as she woke up the next morning, she knew something was wrong. "I could just feel it," she said. "I looked over and I knew Kevin was gone. He died in his sleep of a heart attack at age forty-four."

Now, she says, this heartbreaking experience has taught her not to take relationships, people, or time for granted. "After Kevin died, I looked back at our lives and saw everything so differently. That was our last kiss, our last meal, our last vacation, our last hug, and our last laugh together. I realized you never know, until after the fact, which was the last evening out, the last Thanksgiving. And there will be 'lasts' in all relationships. I want to look back on all those events and feel like I did my best to be fully present, not just half there. I understand that Kevin was a gift I could keep for a while, but not forever. This is true for everyone I meet. Knowing this makes me take in these moments and people even more."

We will have many relationships in our lifetimes. Some—spouses, significant others, friends—we choose, while others, such as parents and siblings, are chosen for us.

Relationships offer us the biggest opportunities for learning lessons in life, for discovering who we are, what we fear, where our power comes from, and the meaning of true love. The idea that relationships are great learning opportunities may seem odd at first, because we know that they can be frustrating, challenging, even heartbreaking experiences. But they can also be, and often are, our greatest opportunities to learn, grow, love, and be loved.

We tend to think that we have relationships with relatively few people, primarily our spouses or significant others. The truth is that we have relationships with everybody we meet, be they friends, relatives, coworkers, teachers, or clerks. We have relationships with the doctors we see only once a year and the annoying neighbors we do our best to avoid. These are all relationships, individual in their own ways yet sharing many characteristics because they emanate from us. You are the common denominator in every single one of your relationships, from the closest and most intense to the most distant. The attitudes you bring to one relationship—positive or negative, hopeful or hateful—you bring to them all. You have the choice of bringing a little or a lot of love to each of your relationships.

❖EKR

Hillary, now on her fourth admission to the hospital, had spent the past few years dealing with her cancer, its treatments and recurrences. Her best friend, Vanessa, and Vanessa's husband, Jack, shared with me that they could accept that Hillary was dying. But Jack said it was so sad that she had not found her special someone and would die alone.

I replied, "She will not die alone. You will be there."

On my next visit to Hillary, Vanessa and I walked out to the hallway to talk because so many visitors were in the room. She said, "Jack had thought it was so sad that Hillary had not found the love of her life, but I am envious of all the love in that room. I had no idea how many people loved her. I don't think I've ever sensed so much pure love for one person. I think it's surprising Hillary, too."

Later that evening, Hillary looked around the room, took in all the faces, and said, "I can't believe all these people are here to see me. I never knew you all loved me so much." Those were her last words.

Some of us may never find that someone special, but that doesn't mean we won't find special love in our lives. The lesson is that we don't always recognize love because we categorize it, declaring romantic love to be the only "real" kind. So many relationships, so much love all around us. We should all be so lucky to live and die with the kind of love that Hillary was surrounded by.

There's no such thing as an insignificant or accidental relationship. Every meeting, encounter, or exchange, with everyone from a spouse to an anonymous telephone operator, no matter how brief or profound, how positive, neutral, or painful, is meaningful. And in the grand scheme of things, every relationship is potentially important, for even the most trivial encounter with a passing stranger can teach us a great deal about ourselves. Every person we encounter holds the possibility of sending us to happiness, to a loving place in the mind, or to a place of struggle and unhappiness. They all have the possibility of bringing us great love and great relationships where we least expect to find them.

We demand a lot from our romantic relationships: healing, happiness, love, security, friendship, gratification, and companionship. We also want them to "fix" our lives, to lift us out of depression or bring us incredible joy. We're especially demanding of these relationships, expecting them to make us happy in every way. Many of us even believe that finding that someone special will improve all aspects of our lives. We don't often think this openly or consciously, but when we examine our belief systems, we find that the thought is there. Haven't you ever once thought something like "If only I were married, everything would be great"?

It's one thing to view romantic relationships as wonderful, as sometimes challenging yet desirable experiences. They remind us of our unique perfection in the world, that we are not in any way broken. Problems arise when we mistakenly believe that they will "fix" us. Relationships cannot and will not fix us; it's fairy-tale thinking to believe so. Yet, it's no surprise that many of us engage in fairy-tale thinking. We are, after all, raised with fairy tales, often encouraged to believe that finding Prince Charming or the girl whose foot fits into the glass slipper will make us whole and complete. We're left with the impression that every frog needs to be a prince. We're subtly taught that until we find that someone special, we are just half a shell, part of a puzzle seeking completion.

Fairy-tale thinking is magical, fun, and has its place. But too much lets us off the hook, relieving us of the responsibility of making *ourselves* happier or better, of handling problems with our careers or families, of dealing with all the other problems of life. Instead, it lets us believe that wholeness, completeness, and solutions will spring from someone special.

A lanky construction worker named Jackson was living as best he could after being diagnosed with leukemia. Shortly after being diagnosed, he met and fell in love with Anne. After a brief courtship they married, and now, two years later, she was nursing him through what was thought to be his final year.

Anne was so proud of their two years together. She said, "I never thought I would be able to love another person so deeply. I was so afraid of commitment, but now I've been able to make the ultimate commitment. I never lasted more than a year in a relationship until I met Jackson. Because of his illness, I've been able to push through all my blocks. In loving Jackson, I finally feel whole."

Then the best—and the worst—thing happened. After failing numerous other therapies, Jackson became eligible for a bone marrow transplant. It worked. Jackson was delivered from a death sentence to remarkable health. Within six months, you would never have guessed he had had leukemia. But now the relationship was quite ill. Anne felt smothered and possessed; she complained that the passion was gone. Her experience is not surprising in relationships that are formed when one partner is quite ill and thought to be headed toward the end of life.

Sensing the change in her, Jackson confronted Anne.

"You were prepared to love and honor me, to be my wife until death do us part—but apparently only if I was going to die in six months. Well, I didn't die, and now this is a real relationship, a real marriage for life. Now that there's no death sentence hanging over me, we're left with the day-to-day commitments, the usual problems everyone deals with. I'm happy I've been given the gift of life. You act like you've been given a life sentence.

"The fairy-tale ending has come true. I am going to live after all, but there are no magic solutions to being in a marriage. We have to really figure out our problems and our marriage. It is much harder to make the day to day work when 'till death do us part' could be fifty years away."

After a confusing struggle with her feelings, Anne went into therapy to try to sort things out. There she learned how it was easier to commit in loss. She said, "Jackson was right. I had just fooled myself again, I had made yet another short-term commitment. I saw how it was one thing to be the hero, the woman who came along at the end of Jackson's life, and quite another to be his wife when he was going to live. I saw how I had tried to use the relationship to fix me, to help me have a successful relationship. Thanks to Jackson's courage to be himself and tell me the truth, I learned that the magic only lies in the day-in-and-day-out experiences we have over the long haul with one another. Jackson's illness pushed me to a deeper sense of commitment. After all we've been through, I realized he really did have my heart. I found the passion again, without the drama of life and death."

Connecting with another person caused Anne to look deeper within herself. It was an incredible lesson about the parts of herself she needed to heal, a tumultuous illustration of what real life is. She exchanged her fantasies for real life and real love, instead of fairy tales and heroes.

Wholeness and completeness must come from within you. Finding that someone special won't cure issues with intimacy or commitment problems. It won't make you happier at work, won't get you that raise, won't make your grades shoot up, won't make the neighbors or city hall any nicer. If you were an unhappy single person, you'll be an unhappy spouse. If you were unable to settle into a career, finding that someone special will make you a careerless person with a partner. If you were a poor parent, you'll be a poor parent in a relationship. And if you felt that you were nothing without Mr. or Ms. Right, those feelings of nothingness will eventually surface in the relationship. The wholeness and completeness you seek are in you, waiting to be discovered.

The search for wholeness in someone to love is based in the concept that we're not enough, we're not complete, we can't generate our own love, we can't create our own happiness in our personal, social, and work lives. The real answer lies in ending the search and completing ourselves. Instead of trying to find someone to love, let's make ourselves more worthy of being loved. Instead of trying to get the partners we already have to love us more, let's become worthier of being loved. And let's ask ourselves if we are giving as much love as we wish to get, or if we expect people to love us dearly even if we're not so lovable and giving. As the saying goes, if your own boat doesn't float, no one will want to sail across the ocean with you.

If you are looking for love, remember that a teacher will appear when you are ready for the lesson. When it is time for you to be in a relationship, that "someone special" will appear. There is nothing wrong with wanting a companion in life, but there's a difference between desiring a loving, joyful relationship and needing someone to complete yourself. You were meant to find great joy and happiness with others. You were also meant to find a sense of wholeness and completion on your own. Someday, you will probably find that someone special. Meanwhile, you are worthy and lovable, just as you are, on your own. You already deserve to be happy, to be a great friend, to get that good job and all the other wonderful things life has to offer.

Always remember that you are something special, just because you are. You are a precious, unique gift to the world, whether you are successful in a career or not, whether you're married to the perfect mate or are on your own. You needn't wait until that external thing comes or happens; you are already whole. The solution doesn't lie in romance. Whether you're married or not, if you want more romance in your life, fall in love with the life you have.

People in intimate relationships usually have the same issues, but in reverse. If you struggle with love, you'll attract someone who has mirror issues with love. If one partner tries to dominate, the other may be passive. If one partner is an addict, the other may be the rescuer. If the shared issue is fear, one attacks it by skydiving and mountain climbing while the other prefers to keep both feet on the ground and stay out of elevators. Like attracts like, in an "opposite" way.

Someone once explained the phenomenon this way: "In any relationship one person makes pancakes, the other one eats them." Typically, when a problem occurs, one partner wants to be more proactive, talk it out, get in there, and work it out. The other, however, prefers to approach it differently, to step back, think, and reflect on it. Each of you thinks the other has a problem, neither of you likes the

way the other handles it. But in a very real sense you're perfect for each other: her more direct approach to the problem pushes all his buttons, and his "refusal" to deal with it
actively pushes hers.

You are always moving toward healing all those places in
you that are wounded. But the progress is not always obvious or smooth. Love will deliver everything unlike itself to
your doorstep for healing. If we ask the universe to make us
more loving, it may not send loving people to us that day.
Instead, it may bring hard-to-love people into our lives. As
we struggle to deal with these people, we have the opportunity to become more loving. So often, the very people we
find ourselves with in relationships push our buttons like
no one else can. Frustrating as these people are, they may be
just the ones we need—the "wrong" people can often be our
greatest teachers.

A strong, outspoken woman named Jane, standing at the
end of life, shared how she had felt victimized by an abusive,
alcoholic father. "And then I chose a husband who turned
out to be abusive and a practicing alcoholic. I ended up leaving that marriage. Looking back, I can see that as painful as
it was, marrying him was the best thing for me. I had to go
back and visit all those feelings of being victimized as a child.
I had a lot of healing to do, and that marriage brought all
those issues to the surface. Now I am deeply grateful for it."

This is also true for those in our life we didn't choose,
often our families. Our parents, siblings, and children, especially teenagers, can upset us in ways no one else can. Difficult as they sometimes are, these relationships are special
teachers of lessons, because we can't disconnect as easily as
we can from friends or others we have chosen. We often
have no other choice but to find a way to work it out. We

may find that the solution is simply to love them, just the way they are.

The situations presented in relationships will bring us all the lessons we need to learn. Like diamonds in a tumbler, we polish each other's rough edges in our relationships.

We sometimes tell ourselves that we'll be happy when certain things about our relationship change. We wish for this because we want the relationship to make us happy. We think that when we change them or the relationship, we'll have the perfect spouses and we'll be happy. That's baloney.

Our happiness does not rely on relationships changing for the "better." The truth is that we can't change other people, and we're not supposed to. What if they never change? What if they're not supposed to change? And if we want to be who we really are, shouldn't we allow them to be who they really are?

Our relationships are not "broken." And that the other people are not being what we want them to be doesn't mean that they are "broken." All relationships are reciprocal, meaning that we mirror our relationship partners. Since like attracts like, we attract what's inside of us.

Charles and Kathy have been married for five years. Charles understood the bad news about the mirror concept. "If I'm in a boring relationship, it may be because I'm bored. Or even worse, I'm boring."

Yes, Charles is right. But the good news is that it makes the problem more tangible. To say that the relationship is boring is not very tangible and leaves it—the relationship—the problem.

The good news is that the issue is inside of you, so it can be reached and worked on. Remember that it's never about letting the others know they are wrong so they will change.

Neither is it ever about making the other person better—it's always about you. You create your own destiny. It is for us to see what lessons lie in the problems before us. Too many times we get rid of our partners instead of the problems. These partners present us with a unique opportunity to see our issues and ourselves. That doesn't mean you should remain in an abusive relationship. But before tossing a partner aside, ask yourself if the problem lies in the partner, in the relationship, or in you.

Looking at the other person keeps us distracted from our real work in the relationship—ourselves. As the saying goes, "How empty of me to be so full of you." The only person we control is ourself. If we work on that person, the circumstances as we see them usually change on their own. This may mean that the relationship is working. Or, it may mean that we see, for the first time, that this relationship doesn't work and it's time for us to move on. It is always an "inside" job.

Several times, when asking people if they want to be in love, we have been surprised by the instant, emphatic replies: "Yes, forever!" or "No, never! Love means giving up my career, sacrificing myself, and always pleasing another person."

The first response is sweet, if possibly unrealistic, but the second is equally disturbing. Is "tremendous sacrifice" really the definition of love? Or is this what these people learned about love when they were young? We model the relationships we see and study as children. Being surrounded by unhappy relationships when we're young can color our attitudes toward love and relationships for the rest of our lives.

We have to look at our relationships and ask, "Is the love I give and receive based on how love was defined for me when I was a child? Is this the kind of love I wish to give and receive? Is it the kind of relationship I really want?" If we see love as being painfully complicated, we must examine why.

If we are thinking love means entanglement, we probably saw entangled relationships as children.

If we think love means abuse, we probably saw abusive relationships.

If we think love means sharing joyfully, we probably saw joyful, sharing relationships.

If we think love means caring for someone lovingly, we probably saw loving, caring relationships.

Unfortunately for some—for too many—what we think of as love is often really control or manipulation, and sometimes even hate. But we needn't be stuck forever in the craziness created by unhappy definitions. We can redefine love for ourselves, we can create the relationships we wish to have. Unfortunately, we don't often do so. Instead, we remain in unhappy relationships, wishing that something would magically happen. Just as some people throw away the partner instead of the problem, others remain in the problem.

We stay in relationships that don't work for two reasons. First, because we hope they will change, and second because we were taught that every relationship should work out. How many times have you known or heard about people going back to old relationships that didn't work? How many times have you heard about a woman going back to a man who has told her that he won't make a commitment? If you're looking for a commitment, why go back to the person with a commitment problem? Why go back to a dry well?

When people are frustrated in repeat relationships, it's as if they're looking for milk in a hardware store. No matter how many times they go up and down the same aisles, they're not going to find any milk. If you want love, tenderness, and affection in your relationships, but you have chosen a person who clearly can't give it to you, it's time to choose someone else. Don't allow people to be reckless with your love, your heart, and your tenderness. And don't allow old definitions to dictate your present life. You can rewrite the rule book by learning to honor yourself and others, and by recording over the old tapes. You can find a new definition of love for yourself, one that truly means treating the other person as valuable, as worthy of great love and care. And you can expect that same treatment for yourself. Whatever it is, it is yours to define for yourself this lifetime.

Besides defining love, we must learn to love without illusions. If our relationships are pure, if we allow the universe to work, and if we get the lessons as they come, our relationships will eventually be built on giving, free-flowing participation and sharing from both parties. Once we let go of trying to change them, we can feel the power of love, without illusions. You don't have to plan, fight, struggle, manipulate, and control. No more "I'm afraid if I don't control him, he won't do it" or "She won't be who I want her to be if I don't change things." We must learn to share our truths with one another. There is nothing wrong with confronting another about something that we find upsetting. But *confrontation with expectation is manipulation*. We must share, we must speak our truth, but not simply to get the reaction we want.

As long as we cling to our agendas and our illusions, we do not truly love. Let them be who they are. If they leave, it might be because they were supposed to go.

Living each day as if we were on the edge of life reminds us that we have "pictures of how it should be." How many times has someone been happy in a relationship today, but wound up fighting over "Will you still be here in twenty years?" Maybe they will, perhaps they won't; the future is not for us to know.

It can be difficult to see people in the present, rather than to focus on the past or future. How many times have we held on to the memories of something they did a long time ago? How often have we let those unhappy memories color our opinion of them today, even though they've apologized and changed? We have our agendas, we still want to punish them or to make them see the past hurt. We hold on to our feelings, accumulating resentments and gathering evidence against those that we love. If we hold on to the past hurts, we no longer have the intention of loving them. Instead of holding on to these unpleasant feelings, we must learn to say "ouch" when we are hurt, and to the person who hurt us. Then we can move on.

When we let go of the future pictures and illusions of how things should look, of our strategies and agendas, love takes on a life of its own. It goes where it wants to go, as opposed to where we try to direct it. We were never really successful in directing love, anyway. When we let go, love can take us to some wonderful and tender places we could never have imagined for ourselves.

Not all relationships are supposed to last a lifetime; some are supposed to end. Some are supposed to last fifty years, others six months. Some relationships are only complete when a person dies; others complete themselves during our lifetimes. The length of a relationship, or how it ends, is never wrong. It's simply life. Ultimately, we have to look at relationships in terms of whether or not they are complete, and of how to best complete them.

Just as we judge death as a failure, we feel relationships have failed if they do not last. The same way we say the only complete and successful life is one that lasted ninety-five years, we feel that the only successful and complete relationships are those that last forever. The reality is that relationships are successful and heal us even if they only last six months. They do what they are supposed to. When they are no longer needed, they are complete and successful.

Unfortunately, we don't always know that relationships are complete and successful. James, who hoped he could make every relationship "work," described his unsettled feelings about a relationship: "My friend Beth and I had a relationship. Two years ago, it ended. I never felt we were supposed to be together, but I did feel that we failed at having a relationship. I was hurt, angry, and sad, and so was she. A month ago, for four straight days, I kept running into people who said, 'I saw Beth last night.' I ran into her coworker, her best friend. My mind immediately said this means something. Maybe I'm supposed to call Beth, maybe the relationship wasn't supposed to end. So I called her and we went out to dinner. At dinner, we never talked about the possibility of getting together again. Instead, we talked about how much we had learned from one another, and how we would be better people in our next relationship because of the one we had had together. Amazingly, the evening shifted my mind from seeing our relationship as a failure to seeing it as successful and complete."

People recycle in our lives. Sometimes this happens because we're not done with the relationships, there's more healing to be done. However, sometimes people recycle because while the relationship is over, we have not completed it in our minds. We need to do our final work on the ending. Sometimes that just means changing our perception of the relationship as incomplete or failing.

There are no mistakes in relationships; everything unfolds the way it's supposed to. From our first encounter with one another to our last good-bye, we are in relationships with each other. We learn through them to see our souls, with their rich topography, and to deliver ourselves to healing. When we let go of our preconceived agendas in loving relationships, we set aside questions of whom we will love and for how long. We transcend these limits to find a love that is magical and created by a force greater than us, just for us.

CHAPTER FOUR

THE LESSON OF LOSS

❖ EKR

A psychology student working to complete his Ph.D. was struggling with losing his seriously ill grandfather, who had helped raise him. Part of the struggle, he said, was deciding whether he should take a leave of absence from his last year of studies to spend more time with his grandfather. But he also felt compelled to complete his schooling now, because he was learning so much about life in this last year of study. "What I'm learning now in school," he explained, "is truly helping me grow as a person."

I said to him, "If you truly want to grow as a person and learn, you should realize that the universe has enrolled you in the graduate program of life, called loss."

We eventually lose everything we have, yet what ultimately matters can never be lost. Our houses, cars, jobs, and money, our youth and even our loved ones, are just on loan to us. Like everything else our loved ones are not ours to keep. But realizing this truth does not have to sadden us. To the contrary, it can give us a greater appreciation for the many wonderful experiences and things we have during our time here.

In many ways, if life is a school, loss is a major part of the curriculum. As we experience loss, we also experience those we love—and sometimes even strangers—caring for us in our time of need. Loss is a hole in our heart. But it is a hole that calls forth love and can hold love from others.

We enter the world suffering from the loss of our mother's womb, the perfect world that created us. We are thrust into a place where we're not always fed when we are hungry, where we don't know if Mom will come back to the crib. We enjoy being held, and then we're suddenly put down. As we get older, we lose our friends when we or they move away, we lose our toys when they break or get lost, and we lose the softball championship. We have our first loves, only to lose them. And the series of losses has just begun. In the years that follow we lose teachers, friends, and our childhood dreams.

All the intangibles—such as our dreams, youth, and independence—will ultimately fade or end. All of our belongings are just on loan to us. Were they ever really ours? Our reality here is not permanent; neither is our ownership of anything. Everything is temporary. Trying to find permanence is impossible, and we ultimately learn that there is no safety in trying to "keep" everything. And there is no safety in trying to prevent loss.

We don't like to see life this way. We like to pretend that we will always have life and the things within it. And we don't want to look at the ultimate perceived loss, death itself. It is amazing to see the pretenses many families of the terminally ill carry on at the end of life. They don't want to talk about the losses they are going through, and they certainly don't want to mention it to their dying loved ones. The hospital personnel don't want to say anything to their patients, either. How shortsighted of us to think that these people approaching the end of their lives are not aware of the situation. And how foolish of us to think that this actually helps them. More than one terminally ill patient has looked at his or her family and said sternly, "Don't try to hide from me that I'm dying. How can you not say it? Don't you realize that every living thing reminds me that I'm dying?"

The dying know what they are losing and understand its value. It's the living who often kid themselves.

✤D K

I learned about loss when I woke up in the middle of the night writhing in pain. I knew from the moment the pain hit that it was serious: this abdominal pain was much more than a standard stomachache. I saw my doctor, who prescribed an antacid and suggested we monitor the problem. Three days later, on a Thursday, the pain was much worse, so my doctor decided to take a closer look. He admitted me to the hospital for the day for a series of tests, including upper and lower GI studies with scopes that allowed him to see if anything in my gastrointestinal tract was abnormal.

In the recovery room, the doctor explained that he had found a tumor partially obstructing my upper intestines.

"Does this mean surgery?" I asked, alarmed.

"I took a biopsy and sent it to the lab," he answered. "We'll know on Monday."

Even though I knew the tumor was just as likely to be benign as malignant, my mind and emotions went to my father, who had died of colon cancer. While waiting four excruciating days for the test results to come back, I mourned the loss of my youthful invulnerability, my health, even my life. The growth turned out to be benign, but the feelings of loss in those few days were very real.

Most of us fight and resist loss throughout our lives, not understanding that life is loss and loss is life; life cannot change and we cannot grow without loss. There's an old Jewish saying that if you dance at a lot of weddings, you'll cry at a lot of funerals. This means if you're present at many beginnings, you'll also be there for many endings. If you have many friends, you'll experience your share of losses.

If you feel that you're suffering great loss, it's only because you have been so richly blessed by life. The losses we experience in life are both big and small, everything from the death of a parent to misplacing a phone number. Life's losses may be permanent, such as death, or temporary, as when you miss your children on a business trip. The Five Stages—which describe the way we respond to all losses, not just death—can be applied to our losses in life, whether big or small, permanent or temporary. Suppose your child is born blind; you might feel it's a major loss and respond this way:

- Denial—The doctors say he can't follow objects with his eyes. Give him time, he'll be able to do it when he gets older.
- Anger—The doctors should have known about this, they should have told us sooner! Why would God do this to us!
- Bargaining—I'll be able to deal with this as long as he's teachable and can take care of himself when he's grown up.
- Depression—This is terrible, his life will be so limited.
- Acceptance—We will deal with the problems as they arise, and he can still have a good life filled with love.

On a more trivial note, suppose you drop a contact lens. You might respond to your loss in this way:

- Denial—I can't believe I dropped it!
- Anger—Darn it, I should have been more careful.
- Bargaining—I promise if I find it this time, I will be much more careful in the future.
- Depression—I am so sad I lost it, now I will have to buy another.
- Acceptance—It's okay, I was bound to lose a contact someday. I'll order a new one in the morning.

Not everyone goes through these five stages with every loss, the responses don't always occur in the same order, and you may visit stages more than once. However, we do experience loss many times, in many ways, and we react to our losses. With loss comes experience of its terrain, making us better equipped to cope with life.

Whatever you are feeling when you lose someone or something is exactly what you are supposed to be feeling. It is never our place to tell someone, "You have been in denial too long, it is now time for anger," or anything like that, for we don't know what someone else's healing should look like. Losses feel just as they feel. They leave us feeling empty, helpless, immobilized, paralyzed, worthless, angry, sad, and fearful. We don't want to sleep, or we want to sleep all the time; we have no appetite or we eat everything in sight. We may bounce from extreme to extreme or we may touch on everything in between. Being in any or all of these places is part of healing.

Perhaps the only certainty about loss is that time heals all. Unfortunately, healing is not always direct; it's not like an ascending line on a graph, quickly and smoothly carrying us up to wholeness. Instead, the process feels something like being on a roller coaster—you climb toward wholeness then suddenly plunge into despair; you seem to regress, then you move forward; then you feel you're back at the beginning. That is healing. You *will* heal, you *will* return to wholeness. You may not get back what you have lost, but you can heal. And at some point on your journey through life, you will see that you never really had in the way you thought that person or item you were mourning. And you will see that you will always have them in other ways.

We long for wholeness. We hope that we can keep people and things just as they are, but we know we can't. Loss is one of our most difficult lessons in life. We try to make it easier, we even romanticize it, yet the pain of separation from someone or something we care about is one of the hardest things we will ever experience. Absence does not always make the heart grow fonder; sometimes it makes us feel sad, lonely, and empty.

Just as there is no good without bad, or light without dark, there is no growth without loss. And odd though it may sound, there also is no loss without growth. This is a difficult concept to comprehend, which is perhaps why we are always struck by it.

Some of the best teachers of this concept are parents who have lost their children to cancer. Typically, parents say the experience is the end of their world, which is understandable. Years later, some will report that they have grown through their tragedies. Of course, they would rather not have lost their children, but they can see how their losses helped them in ways they didn't expect. They have learned that " 'tis better to have loved and lost than never to have loved at all."

And the truth is, we would rarely trade the experience of having and losing our loved ones with never having had them at all.

From a first glance at our lives and losses, it can be hard to see how we've grown. But grow we do. Those who suffer losses ultimately become stronger, more whole.

- In middle age we may lose some of our hair but realize that what's inside is just as important as what's outside.
- In retirement we may lose income, but we find more ˙freedom.
- In old age we may lose a little independence, but we receive back some of the love we gave to others.
- Oftentimes when we lose the possessions of life, we find after mourning that we are freer, realizing that we were meant to travel lightly through this world.
- Sometimes when relationships end, we learn who we are—not in relation to other people, but just as ourselves.
- We may lose some items or abilities, only to realize how much we appreciate that which we have left.

❖EKR

When we think of loss, we think of big losses, such as losing a loved one, our life, our home, or our money. But in the lessons of loss you find that sometimes the small things in life become the big things. Now that my life is confined to the hospital bed in my living room and the chair next to it, I am grateful that I haven't lost some of the things most of us take for granted. With the help of a bedside commode, I can at least go piddle for myself. To me, it would be an enormous loss if I couldn't go to the bathroom on my own, if I couldn't take a bath by myself. Now I'm grateful for just being able to still do these things for myself.

✢ ✢ ✢

Losing those we love to death is certainly one of the most heartbreaking experiences. An interesting comment, made with no disrespect to anyone, is that people who lose someone through divorce or separation will often say that they realize death is not the ultimate loss. Rather, it's the separation from loved ones that is so difficult. Knowing about someone's continued existence but being unable to share it with them may cause far more pain and make resolution far more difficult than permanent separation through death. With those who have died, however, we find new ways to share their existence as they live on in our hearts and memories.

From those who are dying, we have learned some interesting things about loss. Some common, clear lessons come to us from those who have technically been dead but were brought back to life. First, they share that they are no longer afraid of death. Secondly, they say they now know that death is only the shedding of a physical body, no different from taking off a suit of clothes one no longer needs. Third, they remember having a profound feeling of wholeness in death, feeling connected to everything and everyone, and experiencing no sense of loss. Lastly, they tell us that they were never alone, that someone was with them.

✤EKR

A man in his thirties told me that his wife had unexpectedly left him. He felt absolutely devastated. He spoke about the anguish he was going through, then looked up at me and asked, "Is this what loss feels like? Lots of my friends have lost people to breakups and divorces, and even death. They were sad and they told me they were hurting, but I had no concept that it felt like this. Now that I know what it's really like, I want to go back to all those people and say, 'I'm sorry, I had no idea what you were going through.'

"I've grown and become much more compassionate. In the future, when a friend is dealing with a loss, I will be a completely different person, much more helpful to them. I will be there for them in ways I would never have thought of before and understand the pain they are going through in a way I could never have imagined."

This is one of the purposes loss serves in our lives. It unifies us. It helps deepen our understanding of each other. It connects us to one another in a way that no other lesson of life can. When we are joined in the experience of loss, we care for one another and experience one another in new and profound ways.

The only thing as difficult as loss is wondering if there is going to be a loss. Patients often say, "I wish I would either get better or die!" Or, "The days spent waiting for lab tests are excruciating."

A couple struggling to reunite complains, "The separation is killing us. We wish we could make this work—or finally end it."

Life sometimes forces us to live in limbo, not knowing if we will experience loss. We may have to wait hours to hear if the surgery went well, a few days to see the test results, or an indeterminate period as a loved one struggles with disease. We may wait in limbo for hours, days, weeks, or longer when a child is missing. The families of soldiers missing in action are often wrenched by the living in limbo. Decades later, many have still not resolved their losses. They may not be able to, not until they learn that their loved ones are definitely dead, or rescued. But that information may never come. The nation felt the strain of limbo when John F. Kennedy Jr.'s plane was reported missing for a number of days. The local, state, and federal governments threw their resources into finding out what had happened, because we needed closure.

Being in the limbo of possible loss is, itself, a loss. No matter what the outcome of the situation, it is still a loss to be dealt with.

❖DK

I remember my father well: his bright face, the spark in his eyes, the warm smile, and the gold wristwatch with the black strap that seemed to be a part of his arm. I had never known a time when Dad and that watch were not in my life. My father knew I had always loved his watch.

Years ago, as my father was dying, I sat by his bedside, looking at him with tear-filled eyes as I said, "I don't know how to say good-bye to you."

My father replied, "I don't know how to say good-bye to you, either. But I do know that I have to say good-bye to you and everything I have ever loved. Everything from your face to my home. I even looked out the window last night and said good-bye to the stars. Take my watch off," he requested, pointing to his wrist.

"No, Dad. You've always worn it."

"But it's now time for me to say good-bye to it, and for you to wear it."

I gently took the watch off his wrist and placed it on my own. As I gazed down at it, Dad said, "You will have to say good-bye to it someday, too."

As the years passed, I never forgot those words. The watch has always been a bittersweet reminder of the temporariness of life. I rarely take it off. About a month ago I had a hectic day at work, then went to the gym with a friend. I showered at the gym, came home, did some work outside, showered again, and got dressed to go out for the evening. Upon going to sleep that night, I realized the watch was gone. For the next few days I searched everywhere.

I was simultaneously dealing with the loss of the watch that so strongly represented my father and my childhood, and the lesson about loss he had taught me. I had always known I would lose this watch someday, either through my own death or some other circumstances. I really had to sit with the feeling and the knowledge of how temporary everything we have is, how it is truly on loan to us. As time went on, I got used to this concept and the inevitable loss that had occurred. Instead of focusing exclusively on the watch, I found other ways I was connected to my father and my childhood. I made peace with my father's reminder that I, too, would say good-bye to everything someday.

Three months later, I spilled a glass of water on my nightstand. When I leaned over the bed to clean it up, I found the watch. It had fallen behind a bed railing. It is now back on my wrist, but I really understand that all our gifts are temporary. And in this saying good-bye to all, we find something inside ourselves that does not get lost.

Most things we own mean something to us not because of anything actually in the things themselves. Instead, they mean so much to us because of what they represent—and what they represent is ours forever.

❖ ❖ ❖

Loss is complicated and rarely occurs in a vacuum, and no one can predict the response to loss. Grief is personal. The feelings can be conflicted, delayed, and overwhelming.

One loss, or even one possible loss, touches many lives: the family, the friends, the coworkers, and the health care professionals taking care of the patient. Everybody hurts, even the pets. Everybody feels loss. It can separate us or connect us.

A woman at a seminar was grieving the loss of her husband, not from death but to divorce. Interestingly enough, she explained how their problems had begun while he was battling cancer.

"When he was in the middle of his treatment, I would be awake at night and watch him breathing," she explained quietly. "I was consumed by the thought of losing him. I would lie awake wondering what I would do the day he stopped breathing. I couldn't bear the thought of what might happen, of losing him. I eventually had a nervous breakdown and ended up leaving the marriage, out of guilt. It's years later now, he's been in great health. I learned from the situation that when someone is facing a life-challenging illness, all the attention is on them. Everything is focused on how they're doing, how they're feeling, is the treatment working, etc. I realized I felt so selfish to have my own feelings, my own fears. I never thought to say, 'Hey, what about me!' That would have felt wrong. I wasn't the patient, who was I to need help when he was the one dying? So I kept my mouth shut until I finally cracked."

Our grief is clearly affected whenever multiple deaths

or other circumstances, such as murder, an epidemic, or suddenness, complicate mourning. We may find ourselves "sidetracked" by anger over the circumstances of the death, by shock over its rapidity, and so on. Actually, I believe that all grief is complicated; rarely is it simple.

❖DK

Years ago, during the first stages of the AIDS epidemic in the early 1980s, Edward lost over twenty people that he loved. Yet, at the time, he felt what he considered to be too small a sense of loss. "I loved them," he said over and over again. "How could I feel so little?"

For fifteen years he was disturbed that he had not felt anything for all those people he had loved and lost. Then one night he suddenly woke up in a panic and frantically searched through the house looking for pictures of those twenty people. All at once, his grief hit like a ton of bricks from out of the blue. He was now strong enough and ready to begin feeling some of those losses, all those feelings that had been saved for him to deal with when he was able to do so.

We experience our losses in our own time and in our own ways. We are given a beautiful grace in denial. We will feel our feelings when it's time. Meanwhile, they are being held safely for us until we're ready. This is often true for children or teenagers who lose parents: they may not experience much grief until they become adults and can handle it.

We can't escape our past. The sorrow of the past is often held in suspense until we are ready for it to find us. Sometimes new losses trigger old ones. And sometimes we don't feel the loss until later in life, when another loss occurs.

Like many other young war brides of the 1940s, Maurine was devastated when she received a telegram from what was then called the War Department, telling her that her husband was dead.

College sweethearts, she and Roland had hastily married before he enlisted in the army, just a few weeks after Pearl Harbor was bombed. Within a year of their marriage he had finished his training as a fighter pilot and was shipped overseas. Then that telegram arrived.

Instead of mourning, the twenty-one-year-old widow quickly moved to a new state, got a job, and began life anew. Two years after Roland had died, Maurine remarried. Over the next several years she gave birth to three daughters, and her past was all but forgotten. Her new husband knew of her lost love, but she never mentioned anything about Roland to her children or new friends, never hung any pictures of him in her house, and never had any contact with Roland's family or with friends who had known them both.

Fifty years passed; her second husband took ill and died. Now all her grief, for both husbands, came gushing out, mingled into a single river of tears and pain. To deal with her feelings, she created two picture montages on the living room wall: one for her first love, the other for her second. This finally enabled her to sort through the different feelings and losses she had experienced.

People are often conflicted about the loss of loved ones, especially parents about whom they had mixed emotions. The major block to their dealing with and moving through the loss is that they can't understand feeling that way about someone they didn't really like. "My mother was so mean to me," one woman said. "She was literally a tyrant. Why do I care that she died?"

In a recent film version of Mary Shelley's famous novel, *Frankenstein,* Dr. Frankenstein gives life to the famous monster without any regard for the creature's happiness or what his life will be like, dooming him to misery and torment. At the end of the story, when Dr. Frankenstein is finally killed, the creature is found crying. When asked why he is crying for the man who brought him such great suffering, the creature replies simply, "He was my father."

We mourn for those who cared for us the way they should have. We also mourn for those who did not give us the love we deserved. I've seen this phenomenon over and over: the severely beaten child in the hospital longs for his mother but cannot see her, because she is in jail for having beaten him. You can grieve fully for people who were terrible to you. And if you need to grieve for them, you should do so. We must take time to mourn and experience our losses, and to acknowledge that those losses cannot be negated even if we think the person did not deserve our love.

Whether loss is complicated or not, we will all heal in our own time and in our own way. No one can ever tell us we should have been healed by now, or that the process is going too rapidly. Grief is always individualized. As long as we are moving through life and have not become stuck, we are healing.

We often unknowingly re-create losses in an attempt to work through them, to do them better, to finally heal them. If we've been hurt by loss, we may find ways to protect ourselves against loss: we detach, we deny, we rescue others, we help them with their hurts so we don't have to feel ours, we become so self-sufficient that we will never need anyone.

❖EKR

When Gillian was about five years old, her parents left her on the steps of an orphanage. Still a young girl, she didn't see this coming and certainly didn't understand what it was about. Now a bright, middle-aged woman, she has become emotionally healthy and self-sufficient. She spoke of her early loss and how it's affected her. She told me she spent much of her life trying to heal that loss, but has now gone on to realize a much more severe problem. "While what I suffered as a child was severe, that was over forty years ago. But I've realized in the last twenty years, no one abandons me the way I abandon myself."

"Can you tell me about that?" I asked.

"For example, I will hope someone will call me to do something on the weekend, but then I either let my machine pick up when they call or if I answer the phone, I instantly start talking about how busy I am. I don't want them to know how lonely I feel. I never give them a chance to invite me out. And if I have the opportunity to make plans for a holiday, I'll somehow manage not to commit to anything, then end up being alone and feeling like no one cares for me."

Why does she do that? We subconsciously put ourselves in situations that remind us of our original losses so that we can heal. Gillian is finally healing; she is realizing that she's the one who now takes care of her. "I am a forty-eight-year-old woman," she insists, "an adult, not the little girl who was left at the orphanage anymore. Children can be victims, but I am not a child anymore. It's my job to make sure I'm doing what I want to do."

If you wonder why you seem to keep meeting people who abandon you, it may be that the universe is sending you people and situations to help you heal your loss. Eventually, you will heal. In fact, the healing is already under way.

But sometimes the lesson in healing an old loss is in realizing that we can't prevent new losses. By guarding against loss, we incur loss. We ensure we don't lose people by keeping them at a distance, but that is a loss in itself.

A married couple was having trouble in their relationship. They both wanted to have children, but the wife kept putting it off. Eventually, it came out that the woman had lost her mother, father, grandfather, and grandmother, all to cancer. She realized that she was unwilling to have children because she was so afraid that she would lose them, or they would lose her. We talked about the fear of loss, pointing out that no one can know the future. And as much as we may want to, we can't prevent loss, we can't create a guaranteed loss-free situation.

This woman could adopt children: that might lessen the chances of her children developing cancer, if the tendency toward the disease was hereditary. But what other hereditary problems would they have? And what was to stop them from dying in a traffic accident?

As for herself, she could adopt all kinds of cancer-prevention practices. She could eat well and exercise, she could go in for more-than-regular checkups. But suppose she died in an earthquake, an accident, or a holdup? It's impossible to find a world where there is no loss. She realized that all of her fears were *possible,* but not *probable.* Accepting that we can thrive in an imperfect world that brings about fear, she decided to go ahead and have a baby.

These situations sound like losses in themselves, or at

least like new or perceived losses bringing up old ones. They are more than that. They are the creation of healing situations. They bring forth the parts in us now that can heal the loss, that maybe didn't exist before. They are a necessary visit to an old hurt. They are a turning back to wholeness and reintegration.

Loss is often an initiation into adulthood. Loss makes us real men and real women. Real friends and real husbands and wives. Loss is a right of passage. Through the fire to the other side of life.

❖ DK

As a young boy, I saw my mother fall down just as she was being discharged from the hospital. It frightened me, so I told my mother she should go back in. She looked down at my scared little face and said, "People fall, and then hopefully they get back up. That is life."

Losses are like falls in many ways. There is something archetypal about loss, whether it is a loss of someone or something, a loss of balance or a fall from grace. We go through the fire. We are changed, something comes out of the fire anew, a diamond no longer in the rough. Society experiences loss, so do families and individuals. At first a family may experience the chaos surrounding a loss. It is dismembered. After the loss it is changed, it is re-membered.

❖ ❖ ❖

There are many steps to healing loss. Feel and acknowledge the loss when you are ready. Let the grace of denial work, remembering that you will feel your feelings when you are supposed to. You will find the only way out of the pain is through the pain. You will understand it when you are ready to. Many times an understanding of loss comes in years, not days or months. You will find that you can accept a world in which the loss has taken place.

In watching people deal with death you will notice much symbolism. At first, you'll see people taking lots of photos of themselves, as if to say, "I was here." Then as their disease progresses, they often come to a new level and quit taking so many photos. They realize even the photo will not last: in the best scenario the pictures will be handed down through the generations to people who never knew them. They find that what matters more is their own hearts and the hearts of their loved ones. They find that part of loss that we can transcend. We can find the genuine parts of ourselves and loved ones that do not get lost. We can even learn that what really matters is eternal and ours forever. The love that you have felt and the love you have given cannot be lost.

❖ D K

Late one evening I was on the cancer floor in a hospital, seeing a patient. There, I spoke with a nurse who was devastated because she had just lost a patient. "This is the sixth person I watched die this week!" she complained. "I can't take it anymore, I can't watch loss after loss after loss after loss. It feels too bottomless. I don't know if it will ever end."

I asked this caring nurse if she could take a few moments to take a walk with me. Before she could reply, I gently grabbed her hand and we walked across a bridge to another wing of the hospital. Turning a corner, we entered the maternity area, where I walked her up to the glass partition that separated us from the newborn babies. I watched her face as she began to look at new life, taking this scene in as if she had never witnessed it before.

"Doing what you do," I said, "you need to come here often to remind yourself that life is not only about loss."

❖ ❖ ❖

Even within our deepest sense of loss, we know that life continues. Despite all the losses and endings that may be bombarding you, new beginnings are all around. In the midst of pain, loss may seem to be never-ending, yet the cycle of life exists all around us. This nurse realized that she had been seeing her work only as loss. She understood that she had forgotten that she was helping to complete the lives that had begun, just like those of these babies, in similar nurseries, many years ago.

CHAPTER FIVE

THE LESSON OF POWER

Carlos, a forty-five-year-old man diagnosed with HIV, was slowly learning the lesson of power as his disease progressed. "First I lost my job, then my disability ran out, then I lost my insurance. Before I knew it, I was living in a shelter, too sick to work. My life had become a nightmare.

"I was going to a clinic for my health care. They told me about a medical study I might be eligible for. I signed up, had the first physical, and began to wait. One week passed, two, then four weeks and then five. I was getting sicker and sicker. Always being told I would hear next week. I needed to keep checking back since I no longer had a phone. After seven weeks, I could barely even walk to the clinic. I got so tired and out of breath that I had to sit down on the curb. I looked down at the street and thought, 'This is it. This is how it will end.'

"This was not the first challenge of my life. I had grown up very poor, doing farmwork. I didn't have my first pair of shoes till I was eleven years old. I had survived so much in my childhood. What had happened to all that courage and determination? I just sat there and cried. I thought, 'Please, not now, not here. I still want to do more, I want to see the millennium.' I had always wanted to be part of both centuries. I cried because I had lost all my power.

"I felt like my soul was shriveling up. I was losing myself. Did I have to die here?

"Then it hit me: I was still here. Was all my power really gone?

"I managed to get up and make it to the clinic. I said to the nurse, 'My body needs help. I don't have time to wait anymore for this study to call me. There must be some other way to get the new drugs.'

"Because I was so insistent, the nurse enrolled me in another program at a different site, which had an opening in their study. That very day, I started on a new combination of medications. Now, two years later, my body has rebuilt itself. I am no longer dying. I can trace it all back to remembering my power that day. If I had not remembered my power, I would have died long ago."

Our real power is not derived from our positions in life, a hefty bank account, or an impressive career. Instead, it is the expression of that authenticity inside of us, our strength, integrity, and grace externalized. We don't realize that each of us has the power of the universe within us. We look around and we see others as powerful, we see nature as powerful, we can witness a seed turning into a flower or the sun crossing the sky every day. We even see life created in us, from us. Yet we see ourselves as disconnected from all of this power. God did not make nature powerful and man weak. Our power comes from the knowledge that we are unique, and from our understanding that we have the same innate power as all other creations. Our power lies deep within us. It is the power with which we were born. If it has been forgotten, it needs only to be recognized again.

Dr. David Viscount told a symbolic story that reminds us how to find and use our power. He described a law that said if you own a piece of property, such as an empty lot, and people cut through it, you must post a sign at least once a year that indicates it is private property. If you do not post a sign, after so many years the land will become public. Our lives are like that property. From time to time we must reassert the boundaries by which we define ourselves, saying "No" or "That hurts" or "I will not let you walk over me." Otherwise we give our power to those who intentionally or unintentionally walk over us. It is our responsibility to take back our power.

In a famous skit, the late comedian Jack Benny played a notorious cheapskate who was accosted by a gun-wielding robber demanding, "Your money or your life!" Jack stood there for a long time before saying, "I'm thinking, I'm thinking."

We tend to equate wealth with power, and we believe that money can buy happiness. Yet it is a sad day for many when they finally have that money but realize that they're not happy. Just as many rich people commit suicide as those who have not accumulated riches. Sigmund Freud once said that given a choice of treating rich or poor patients, he would always choose the rich because they no longer think all their problems will be solved with money. Of course, most of us would still like to experience money. But that's all money is—an experience. Different from but not better than other experiences.

A wise man knew all about money and happiness, because he had both. During a period of financial challenges he was asked, "What is it like being poor?" He replied, "I am not poor, I am broke. Poor is a state of mind and I will never be poor."

He was right, wealth and poverty are states of the mind.

Some people without money feel rich, while some rich people feel poor. Being poor means you are thinking poor, which is much more dangerous than running low on money. You are thinking without worth, forgetting that while money comes and goes, you are always of worth. Thinking abundantly is the opposite of thinking poorly. In remembering your worth, in remembering just how precious and valuable you are, you are increasing your self-worth. That and that alone is the beginning of true wealth. Some of us treat objects as being valuable; that's fine, unless we forget that *we* are even more precious than any object we can acquire.

We are often advised to do what we love, and money will follow. This is sometimes true. What is always true is that if you do what you love, you will have a greater sense of value in your life than if you own a Mercedes. At thousands of deathbeds, thousands of people express their regrets. Many say, "I never followed my dream," "I never did what I truly wanted to do," and "I was a slave to money." No one says, "I wish I had stayed at the office longer" or "I would have been so much happier with another ten thousand dollars."

Just as we believe that money gives us strength, so do we feel that control over people and situations gives us power. The more control we have the better; we must control everything or all will be chaos. Of course, we need to have some control to get through the activities of daily living. Problems arise when we exercise more than a reasonable amount; then we become unhappy, rather than powerful. The more control we grab the less quality we have as we expend all our energy trying to control the uncontrollable.

It's true that those who possess more money or have powerful positions can control their external environments more than those who do not, but that has nothing to do with real power. That's just temporary influence over others. Anything we fear to lose—our body, job, money, and beauty—is a symbol of external power.

When we try to control people and situations, we rob them and ourselves of the natural victories and setbacks that occur in life. We want them to do it our way for their own good. But "our way" is not always best. Why should other people do it our way? Why shouldn't they bring their uniqueness to everything they do? We become more powerful in relationships and life when we let go of control, realizing that we cannot control people, things, or events — that was all an illusion. But life does not become chaotic when we release control. Instead, it falls into the natural order of things.

✤EKR

I once saw the natural order of things unfold perfectly, but in an unusual way.

One day I was giving a lecture in New York to fifteen hundred people. Afterward, hundreds of people stood in line for my signature. I signed as many books as I could, but then I had to leave for the airport. I signed a few more, but knew I had to leave immediately.

I rushed to the airport, only to find that the flight had been delayed fifteen minutes. Fortunately, this gave me time to stop in the bathroom—which I desperately needed to do. While I was in the stall, I heard someone say, "Dr. Ross, would you mind?"

I thought, "Mind what?"

Then, one of my books was pushed under the stall door, along with a pen for signing.

I answered, "Yes, I would mind," and grabbed the book,

thinking I would take my time before coming out of the stall. But I was curious to see who would do such a thing.

A nun was waiting. I said to her, "I will never forget you, for the rest of my life." And I didn't mean that sweetly. I meant, "How dare you not let me use the bathroom in peace!"

She responded, "I'm so grateful, this is God's providence." The woman could tell from the look on my face that I didn't understand what she meant, so she said, "I'll tell you what I meant by that."

I could tell that every word she said was from the bottom of her heart. I hated this situation because I felt "How dare someone try to control and manipulate me this way!" But I realized there was enormous power in her purity. She said, "My friend is a nun who is dying in Albany. She was counting the days until your lecture. She wanted to go so badly, but was too sick to make the journey. I wanted to do something for her so I came, taped your lecture, and wanted to get a signed book for her. I stood in line for over an hour because I knew how much it would mean to her. I was only a few people away from you when you finally had to leave. As much as I tried to do everything within my power to get the signature, I just missed you. Can you understand why, when I saw you come into the bathroom, I knew it was absolute grace, that the universe had brought us to the same airport, the same airline, the same bathroom, at the same time?"

This woman did not know where I was going, if I was leaving town, which airport I was going to, or if I was even flying. She was shocked when she ran into me in the bathroom, which showed me we don't need to control things to make them happen if they're supposed to. There are no accidents, only divine manipulations. That's real power.

❖ ❖ ❖

Our personal power is our inherent gift and our real strength. Unfortunately we often forget it, in many different ways, without realizing it.

We give our power away when we become concerned with other people's opinions. To recapture this power, remember that this is *your* life. What matters is what *you* think. You don't have the power to make *them* happy, but you do have the power to make yourself happy. You can't control what *they* think; in fact, you can rarely influence it much at all. Think back to the people you were trying to please ten years ago. Where are they now? They are probably not in your life today. Or, if they are, you are probably still trying to get their approval. Let it go. Take back your power. Form your own opinion of yourself.

Our power is meant to help us do what we want, to become all we can be. It has not been given to us just so we can do what we "should" do. That is the worst thing we can do with this life. We must fulfill *ourselves*.

Personal power makes room in our lives—and the lives of those around us—for integrity and grace. That power means that we support others in being strong—we are strong enough to give credit rather than taking it. And this kind of power supports us internally. When I see you as strong, I recognize the strength that is within me. When I see you as loving I can't help but respond lovingly, and find the love that's inside me. Ultimately, what I believe about you I end up having to believe about myself. If I believe you are not a victim, it helps me realize that I am not one, either. It is grace that allows this goodness to expand, to reach out. In believing for others, we find the faith to believe for ourselves.

But we are human and often lose our way. We review our mistakes and our lacks, then say, "I am unhappy because of these mistakes I have made. I am not good enough, so I will try to change." But seeing only our mistakes and inabilities binds us to them. We tell ourselves, "I wasn't 'enough' before, but I will be 'more' from now on," thus beginning the dangerous game of "more." We tell ourselves we will be happy when we have more money, when we have more authority at work, or when we are more respected.

Why does tomorrow seem to hold so much more possibility for happiness or power than today? Because we delude ourselves in the game of more, losing our power no matter how we play the game. And the game of more keeps us in a place of lack, feeling not good enough. Should we get what we want, we feel even worse because it's still not enough. We're still unhappy. If only we had a little more. We don't realize that simplicity is what matters.

The dying can no longer play the game of more because, for them, there may be no tomorrow. They discover that there is power in today, and there is enough in today. If we believe in an all-powerful and good God, do we also believe he would say, "I'll have to wait till tomorrow"? God would not say, "I wanted Bill to have a good life, but, oh, well, he has the wrong job so I can't do much." God does not see the limits we put on our lives and ourselves. God has given us a world where life can always get better, not tomorrow, but today. If we allow it to, a bad day can turn into a good day, an unhappy relationship can recover, and many other "wrongs" will turn out right.

Leslie and her five-year-old daughter, Melissa, were walking across the street in a shopping area. A Jeep with music blaring ran the stoplight as it changed lanes to make a left turn. The driver, only seventeen years old, couldn't see Leslie and Melissa because he had turned into the sun.

But Leslie saw the Jeep; she knew they would be hit. She could only grab her daughter in her arms. The driver saw them at the last moment and swerved. He hit some parked cars, coming to stop only inches from the frozen mother and daughter. The young boy was devastated by what had happened, but Leslie could only feel thankful.

"It could easily have ended another way, with Melissa and me lying in the street, dead," the relieved mother said. "Life can take so many directions. I got on my knees that day because we were spared. Since then, I take nothing for granted. Now, when my fifty-five-year-old mother calls and tells me her mammogram was clear, I thank her for getting checked. I thank God for her health. There was something that I realized about the fragileness of life that has fueled my gratitude. That gratitude has given my life enormous meaning and power."

A grateful person is a powerful person, for gratitude generates power. All abundance is based on being grateful for what we have.

True power, happiness, and well-being are found in the fine art of gratitude. Being grateful for what you have, for things just as they are. Having gratitude for who you are, those things you have brought to the world in your birth. Your uniqueness. In one million years there will never be another you. No one can see and respond to the world quite the way you do. On the other hand, if you do not know how to appreciate the things and people you have now, why would you be able to appreciate more things, people, and power when you get them? You won't, because you have never worked on your "gratitude muscle," you never learned or practiced being grateful. Instead you will think, "This second wife, this second million dollars, this bigger house, are still not enough. I need more." And so you will live, continually wanting more or wishing things were different than they are, playing the game of "more" instead of being grateful for all you have.

We focus on our own paths, paths that take us to things greater and grander than money and material wealth; we trade the game of "more" for "enough." We quit asking "Is it enough?" because in our last days we will realize it was enough. Hopefully, we can understand this before our lives come to an end.

When life is "enough," we don't need any more. What a good feeling it is when our days are enough. The world is enough. We don't often let that feeling in. It's a foreign feeling because we tend to live our lives feeling that they are not enough. But we can change that perception. Saying that this is life and I don't need anything more is a wonderful statement of grace and power. If we don't need any more, if we don't need to control everything, we can let life unfold.

We have so much power inside but so little knowledge of how to use it. Real power comes from knowing who we are and our place in the world. When we feel we must accumulate, we have truly forgotten all that we are. We must remember that our power comes from knowing that everything is all right and everyone is unfolding exactly as they are supposed to.

CHAPTER SIX

THE LESSON OF GUILT

❖DK

Years ago, Sandra was delighted when Sheila, her best friend, told her that she was getting married—and ecstatic when Sheila asked her to serve as maid of honor. On the wedding day, twenty-year-old Sandra, driving her brand-new car, arrived to pick up the bride-to-be and take her to the church. Sandra had volunteered for the job not only because she was the maid of honor but also because it meant the bride was going to arrive in style.

It was raining as Sandra pulled into the carport at Sheila's apartment. The maid of honor helped the bride carry wedding clothes and honeymoon luggage to the car and was about to hop into the driver's seat when Sheila said, "Let me drive."

"You can't drive to your own wedding!"

"Let me," insisted Sheila. "It will help me get my mind off a million things, not to mention that the sun has chosen not to attend my wedding."

Sandra gave her best friend the keys, and off they went. They drove the couple of miles toward the church, reviewing wedding details and commenting on how bad the weather was getting, how hard the rain was falling. All of a sudden the car started sliding and Sheila lost control. The car slammed into a lamppost, killing the bride instantly. Sandra suffered a few broken bones, but survived. That is, she survived physically. Her psyche, however, was gravely wounded.

Even now, twenty years later, she is haunted by what happened that day. "If only I had driven," she lamented, "Sheila would still be alive."

In talking to Sandra, I asked her some questions: "Do you absolutely know that Sheila would have survived if you had driven? Did you know there was going to be a car accident? Did you know she was going to die? Did you know you would survive and she wouldn't?" The answer to all these question was no.

"No, but I lived and she didn't!"

It was clear that Sandra was still unable to release her guilt. I asked, "If it had been the other way around and the roles were reversed, what would you want Sheila to say to you? In other words, if you had died and she was here, and you could speak to her, what would you say to her? If you could look down and see your friend, decades later, still haunted by guilt, what would you say to her about the incident?"

Sandra took a minute to really put herself in her friend's place. "I would say, 'I was the one driving, I was responsible for my decisions. No one forced me to drive and no one could have prevented me. It was my wedding day and I wouldn't have taken no for an answer to driving.'" Sandra's eyes filled with tears from a tragic day long since past. "I would say, 'It wasn't your fault. It just happened. I don't want you to waste your life feeling guilty.'"

❖ ❖ ❖

Sometimes events, even the most tragic of events, happen, and it's no one's fault. None of us knows why one person dies and another survives. Sandra was guilt-ridden because she was angry with herself for not driving, because she had let her friend "drive and kill herself." Sandra had to be reminded that, at the time, she did not know—she could not possibly have known—the consequences of their decision as to who would drive. She thought she was helping her friend have a more enjoyable wedding day by letting her drive her new car.

This reaction is often called survivor's guilt, but it is guilt with no logical basis. The concept first got widespread attention after World War II, as some concentration-camp survivors wondered, "Why them and not me?" The phenomenon of survivor's guilt occurs whenever someone witnesses or survives a catastrophic experience, such as the Oklahoma City bombing, plane crashes, car accidents, even widespread diseases such as AIDS. It may also strike when a loved one dies, even from natural causes. Although it is easy to understand why people who have lived through painful or horrific events would wonder why they had been spared, it is ultimately a question without an answer. There is even unknowing arrogance in our asking the question. It is not for us to ask why someone dies or why someone lives; those decisions are for God and the universe to make. And yet, though there is no answer to our question, there is a reason for what has happened: the survivors have been spared in order to live. The real question is this: If you have been spared in order to live, are you living?

The psychology of guilt is rooted in self-judgment, the sense that we have done something wrong. It is anger turned inward, arising when we violate our belief systems.

Much of the time, this unhappy self-judgment is rooted in what we were taught as children. Our guilt so often comes from our childhood because we were raised to be "prostitutes." This sounds harsh, but it's true. Obviously, in using the word *prostitute* I'm talking about how, as children, we symbolically sell ourselves for the affection of others. We are usually taught to be good little boys and girls, tending to the wishes of others rather than forming strong identities for ourselves. We're not really encouraged to be independent or interdependent. We're trained to be *codependent,* making others' needs and lives important and neglecting our own. It is not a conscious choice; often we don't know how to meet our needs for our own happiness.

One clear symptom of this codependency is an inability to say no. We're taught to please others by agreeing to their requests. Many parents are unhappy when their children say no. In fact, it's wonderful when children learn to say no, at the appropriate times. We all should learn to say no— early, loud, and clear.

The desire to please others is a fertile ground for guilt, but not the only one. Sometimes we feel guilty when we try to assert our independence. This can be a particular problem for children who suffer a loss while still forming their identities. It takes a wise parent to help overcome or head off this guilt.

✤ E K R

Nine-year-old Scott was angry with his mother for not letting him go on a camping trip. She had clearly warned him that he could not go unless he completed his homework, but it was hard for Margie to discipline her son. At forty, she had cervical cancer, which had spread to her liver. "I don't want to see him unhappy with me," she explained to me. "We have so little time left."

Despite Margie's desire for harmony, the homework-versus-camping argument became heated. Tommy spat out, enraged, "I wish you were dead."

That's a pretty harsh statement. Others might have snapped back, "Don't worry, you'll have your wish soon," but Margie looked at him and lightly replied, "I know you don't mean that. I do know you are very angry."

Ten months later, now confined to her bed, she adds, "I want to leave Scott with good memories. I know my dying will scar his childhood, if not end it. That's bad enough, but I don't want to leave him with guilt. So I've talked to him about guilt. I said, 'Scotty, do you remember when you were very mad at me and said you wished I was dead? Well, after I am gone a long time, you will remember things like that and you might feel bad. But I want you to know that all kids get mad and sometimes think they hate their mom. I know you don't really hate me. I know you are deeply hurting inside. I don't ever want you to feel guilty about that kind of stuff. You have made being a mother a wonderful experience for me. It was worth living just to be with you.'"

❖ ❖ ❖

Most of us are not as wise as Margie was about guilt and its beginnings. Most of us are unaware of the guilt we instill in our children, and that was instilled in us. Our lives continue into adulthood filled with guilt, and it's loud, punishing, and mostly unproductive.

To some extent we need guilt. Society would be chaotic without it. There would be no red lights telling us to stop. We would drive as if we were the only people on the road.

Guilt is part of the human experience. Guilt can sometimes be a guide, telling us that something is off. It can indicate that we are not following our belief systems, that we are outside the boundaries of our integrity. To move past guilt, we must align our beliefs and our actions.

❖DK

Helen and Michelle, now both in their fifties, had been friends for over two decades. But Helen was now angry with Michelle; they had hardly spoken for over four years. Helen would become irate at the mere mention of Michelle's name: "I still have four years of birthday presents for her in my basement. I am not giving them to her until she finds time for me."

Both, in their second marriages, had become friends in name only. Michelle was the first to get married again. Helen was happy for her, but began to feel unimportant. Just about this time, Helen met her second husband. The two old friends continued to drift apart. Helen would call Michelle to get together, but she never seemed to find the time. Helen would say, "I have your birthday present for you, Michelle, we have got to get together," but they never did.

Now Helen was facing breast cancer. As she reviewed her life, this broken friendship kept coming up. When I asked her why she didn't mail all the birthday gifts she had purchased for Michelle to her old friend, she replied furiously, "Not till we get together. And I have been trying for years now. I keep calling her and telling her about the wonderful gifts I have gotten her."

I asked the angry woman if she thought guilt played a role in her estrangement from her friend. She quickly replied, "I don't feel guilty."

I asked her if she might be trying to make her friend feel guilty. "Why would you think such a thing?" she asked, puzzled.

"It seems to me," I replied, "that for whatever reason, Michelle was ending or at least changing the form of your friendship by not getting together. Rather than confronting this directly, you continued to do or say nothing, except to buy more gifts every year. I can understand the first year, but why continue for four years? You must have realized that you were buying gifts that would just accumulate."

"I kept thinking this year we would find time."

When I asked her if the gifts had changed in any way from year to year, she told me that they had got nicer. I then asked her why she would give nicer and nicer gifts to someone who was not interested in receiving them.

Puzzled, Helen began to think back on her actions. Then she blurted out angrily, "You don't understand. Michelle is wrong, she's the one not willing to get together."

"That may be," I countered. "But are those gifts you bought for her gifts of guilt? When you kept buying nicer and nicer gifts, what did you want Michelle to feel when she opened them?"

Helen looked down, finally admitting quietly, "I wanted her to feel guilty for not getting together with me."

"Don't you think she can hear that in your voice? Maybe that's why she doesn't want to get together with you. You are not offering her friendship anymore; those are gifts of guilt."

"I want to clear this up. I want to do this better."

"Then mail her the gifts."

"No," Helen replied adamantly.

"Then give them to charity."

"No, I can't."

"If you want to feel better, you have to let go of the guilt; the guilt you have, the guilt you are giving. As long as you hold on to those gifts, you are holding on to guilt. You are now feeling guilty because you are trying to make her feel guilty."

"I'll think about it."

A few weeks later, Helen called Michelle one last time. This time, instead of saying "I have gifts for you," she apologized for them. Michelle told her that she had indeed felt she was being held hostage by those gifts. The two are now talking again and working on rebuilding their relationship. They have decided to start "clean," and the gifts were given to charity.

❖   ❖   ❖

Guilt binds us to the darkest parts of ourselves. It is a connection to our weakness, our shame, and our unforgiveness. The smallest part of ourselves feeds on it. Inaction nourishes it. When we feel guilty, we stay small-minded, our lower thoughts are in control. After a while we become ashamed. The remedy is to take action and share our feelings. The real you does not know guilt. Your true self is beyond the guilt of this world.

Shame and guilt are deeply connected. Shame comes from old guilt. While guilt is about what you did, shame is about who you think you are. The guilt that attacked your consciousness becomes the shame that assaults your soul. Like the guilt that precedes it, shame usually takes root in childhood, before we know who we are. It begins to grow before we know we are responsible for our mistakes, and that we will make many of them, but that we *are not* our mistakes. If our needs and our parents clashed, we felt we must have done something wrong. We began to believe we *were* wrong. We buried our hurt, our anger, and our resentment. Now we just feel bad about ourselves.

At fifteen years old Ellen was too young to be a mother, but not too young to get pregnant. Her family never expected anything like this; they had not even discussed the facts of life with her. When Ellen could no longer hide it, she told her parents of her condition. Filled with guilt and shame, Ellen's family sent her away to have the child and put it up for adoption. Ellen refused to have any pain medications during childbirth, for she wanted to "get one good look at my child." She was able to see, but not hold, her precious little daughter before she was taken away.

Now, over fifty-five years later, Ellen has a weakened heart and poor overall health. "It's time to wrap up life," she said. "I accept it just as it was, except for my firstborn daughter. I realize I must forgive myself for giving her up. I was a child myself when it happened. I didn't understand the consequences of my actions. But I see how this shame has been an undercurrent through my whole life. I've thought a lot about my child. I felt incomplete. It is probably too late to find her, and maybe even selfish—she might not even know she was adopted. Even though I was young and didn't know any better at the time, I want to leave this world feeling like I have taken some action to transcend my shame. So I've written my daughter a letter":

By the time you read this, I will probably be gone. While I have had a good life, you were always missing from it. I have spent much of it feeling guilty. I could have resolved things sooner. I don't know if I could have found you, but I could have made it easier for you to find me if you wanted. Now that life is over for me, I have one thing left to do, and that is to leave you this message: If you can find a way to live your life to its fullest despite how unfair it can be, you will end your life with a true sense of worth. I know this is hard to do. I ran into unfairness early in life, but yours began at the very beginning. You can find worth. Not perfection, but worth. I needed to tell you that you were wanted, and that I never wanted to leave you. In some ways I never did leave you. I hope you have a good life, and a meaningful one. If there is a heaven, I will watch over you and protect you in death in a way I never could in life. My deepest wish is that when your times comes, I can come to meet you.

Ellen's letter was found as her family cleaned her room after her death. Her story was reported on a local radio station, so that the letter might find its intended recipient. A few months later a woman came forth to see if she could be Ellen's daughter. After some checking, it was confirmed that she was.

As in Ellen's case, shame in our childhood makes us feel more responsible for our situations than we are. If we were abused, we feel we caused the abuse. If we are ashamed, we feel we deserved the shame. If we were unloved, we feel we are not worthy of love. We feel we are at fault for our bad feelings. The truth is, we are of worth and value. Yes, we may have felt bad about our actions at times, but those feelings actually make us good, for bad people don't feel bad about hurting others. See the best in yourself. Remind yourself of your goodness.

Many spiritual belief systems view guilt as part of a lower thought system—thinking that is apart from God, or thinking that is without love. Our first instinct is to get rid of guilty feelings because they are so painful. We do this unconsciously, by projecting the feeling onto someone else. "Since it is hard for me to feel guilty and wrong, I will see *you* as being guilty and wrong." In other words, it can't be me, so it must be you. But when we hide in that projection, we stay stuck in a cycle of guilty feelings that we cannot resolve.

Peace and guilt are opposites. You cannot experience peace and guilt at the same time. When you accept love and peace, you deny guilt, but the opposite is also true: when you cling to guilt, you turn away from love and peace. The good news is that this is a decision. You can commit to love, you can exchange feelings of guilt for feelings of peace.

Some believe in a God that sees us as bad and unlovable. But many at the edge of life find a God that loves us unconditionally, that sees us as guiltless. Of course we have made mistakes, that is part of the human experience. It is our guilt that keeps us separated from our true reality of love and God.

Guilt and time are closely connected, too. Since guilt always comes from the past, it keeps the past alive. Guilt is a way to avoid the reality of the present. It drags the past into the future: a past of guilt will create a future of guilt. Only when you release your guilt do you truly release your past to create a new future.

Guilt clearly needs to be processed out. Workshops can be extremely helpful in allowing people to release their anger. Then they must share their guilt. If they share it from a place of good intentions, they will release it, sometimes with a flood of tears. This kind of sharing is much like the Roman Catholic confession. When we confess, we release the burden of the secret and often encounter the grace of knowing that we are loved by a power greater than ourselves. We can also learn that we are still worthy of love from others. The key to healing is forgiveness. Forgiveness means acknowledging the past and letting it go.

Anything that you think you are guilty of can be cleaned and purified with forgiveness. You have been hard on others your whole life, and you have been even harder on yourself. Now it is time to release all these judgments. As a holy child of God, you do not deserve to be punished. Once you forgive yourself and others, the guilt is no longer yours to keep. We do not deserve guilt; we deserve forgiveness. When we learn this lesson, we are truly free.

CHAPTER SEVEN

THE LESSON OF TIME

O ur lives are governed by time. We live by it and in it. And of course, we die in it. We believe time is ours to save and to lose. We can't buy time, but we talk about spending it. And timing, we believe, is everything.

Today we know what time it is at every point on the globe, but before the mid–nineteenth century, we measured time more casually. The advent of rail travel made stricter scheduling a necessity, so in 1883 the American and Canadian railroads adopted the system we still use of four time zones in North America. The plan was considered radical: many felt that the time zones and standards of time were insults to God. Today, we accept our watches and alarm clocks as *the* truth. We even have a "national clock" in the Naval Observatory, an "official timekeeper" for the United States. But this "national clock" is actually a computer that averages the findings of fifty different clocks.

Time is a useful measurement, but it has only as much value as we give it. *Webster's* defines time as "an interval separating two points on a continuum." Birth appears to be the beginning and death the ending, but they are not, they are just points on a continuum.

Albert Einstein pointed out that time is not constant, that

it's relative to the observer. And we now know that time passes at different rates depending on whether you are standing still or moving. Time runs differently if you take a trip on a spaceship or even a plane or subway. In 1975 the navy tested Einstein's theory, using two identical clocks; they placed one on the ground and the other in a plane. For fifteen hours the plane flew while lasers were sent between the two clocks comparing time. Just as Einstein had stated, the time was slower in the moving plane. Time is also dependent on perception. Imagine a man and a woman together in a movie theater, watching the exact same movie, except she loves the film while he hates it. For her, the movie ends too soon. For him, it lasts forever. Both he and she agree that the movie started at 7 P.M., and that the final credits rolled at 8:57 P.M. But they don't agree on the experience of that one hour and fifty-seven minutes. In a tangible way, one person's time is not another's.

We wear wristwatches—and synchronize them—to make sure we show up for the meeting, meal, movie, or other activity at the right time. That's good, it makes it easier for us to interact and get things done, it helps us communicate and coordinate. But when we go further, insisting that the arbitrary designation of seconds, minutes, hours, days, weeks, months, and years is time itself, we forget that we all experience time differently because the value of time depends on individual perception.

Think of time as a rainbow. Agreeing to coordinate our lives according to a clock to ensure that we begin and end work at the same time, etc., lets us see one color of the "time rainbow" the same way. But we see all the other colors in our individual ways.

In time, everything changes. We change inside, we change

outside, our looks change, and our inner selves change. Our lives continually change, yet we usually do not like change. Even when we're prepared for it, we often resist it. In the meantime, the world changes around us. It doesn't keep time with us—the changes seem to come either too quickly or too slowly.

Change may be our constant companion, but we don't tend to think of it as our friend. Change scares us because we may not be able to control it. We much prefer the changes we have decided to make—they make sense to us. It's the changes that happen to us that make us uneasy, that make us feel as if life may be going in the wrong direction. But like it or not, change happens and, like most things in life, doesn't really happen *to us*—it just happens.

Change is saying good-bye to an old, familiar situation and facing a new, unfamiliar situation. Sometimes it's not the old or the new that unnerves us, it's the time in between. Ronnie Kaye, author of *Spinning Straw into Gold* and a two-time breast cancer survivor, says, "In life when one door closes, another door always opens . . . but the hallways are a bitch." That is how change works, it usually begins with a door closing, an ending, a completion, a loss, a death. Then we enter an uncomfortable period, mourning this completion and living in the uncertainty of what is next. This period of uncertainty is hard. But just when we feel we can't take it anymore, something new emerges: a reintegration, a reinvestment, a new beginning. A door opens. If you fight change, you will be fighting your whole life. That's why we need to find a way to embrace change, or at least to accept it.

When we ask someone "How old are you?" we are really asking them "What time are you?" We're trying to slap a frame of reference on the person by bringing the past into play. When I find out how old you are, I know what memories you are likely to have. Depending on your age, you may know all about the Marshall Plan, Jackie O., the first moon walk, dial phones, disco, or DOS. I can call this information up in a friendly way, singing old Beatles songs with you. I can bring it back in a hostile way, thinking that you're a fool to have gotten caught up in "flower power." In either case, I'm not seeing you exactly as you are now. I'm judging by what I see as the sum of your past experiences.

It's liberating to step away from perception. We've all heard lines like "You don't look forty," and the reply "This is what forty looks like." The first person is essentially saying "you don't fit my perception." The second person is pointing out that this is what forty years old looks like on me—don't define me by your expectations.

We don't value age in Western culture. We don't see wrinkles as part of life; they're something to be prevented, hidden, removed. Yet as much as we miss the energy and buoyancy of youth, most of us wouldn't want to retrace our steps because we also vividly remember the confusion of those years. We reach middle age with a better understanding of what life is about, and we don't have time for the extraneous nonsense. We know who we are and what will make us happy. Once we have learned this lesson, we would not trade it for our youth again. There is a comfort in this wisdom and in the recollection that youth is many things, not all of them easy. It may be the age of innocence, but it is also the age of ignorance. It is the age of beauty; it is also the age of painful self-consciousness. It is often the age of adventure and, just as often, the age of stupidity. For many the dreams of youth become the regrets of the old, not because life is over but because it was *unlived*. To age gracefully is to experience fully each day and season. When we have truly lived our lives, we don't want to live them again. It's the life that was not lived that we regret.

How many years would we like to live? If we were given the chance to live to be two hundred years old, or to live forever, how many of us would take it? Thinking about this helps us to understand the meaning of our lifetimes. We don't want to live beyond our time: how empty it would feel to continue in a world where things have grown beyond our comprehension and we have lost everyone we love.

✤ EKR

A man shared a story about his ninety-two-year-old mother. "I took her on a vacation to her hometown, Dallas. We were on a new plane. I watched my mother struggling to open the bathroom door, which was fitted with new door handles that were flush with the panel. She was used to knobs and handles with buttons.

"Early the next morning, the fire alarm went off in the hotel. By the time I got to her room she was outside the door in her nightgown, startled. She was also angry, because she had forgotten to grab her magnetic card key and the door had locked behind her. She was in a panic, not sure how she would get back in, not to mention being undressed. After the trip she told me, 'I don't belong here anymore. I don't know how to use a microwave, I can't find a TV with a dial to change the channel, I don't know how to use cards instead of keys, and all my friends are gone. Time has moved on, but I've been left behind.' It was hard to hear. It would have been even harder to understand, but on the trip

I saw how frustrating and complicated life had become for my mother."

❖ ❖ ❖

When we look at the night sky, we are literally seeing the past. We see the sky not as it is tonight, but as it looked years ago, from a few to a million, for that's how long it takes the light from the closest of the distant stars to reach Earth.

We have much the same experience with other people. Think, for example, about the neighborhood troublemaker from when you were young. If you thought he was a problem back then, you will be cautions when you see him today because you will see him as he was, not as he is.

How many of us see our parents as who they are today? That's a pretty big task, given our strong early impression of our parents as all-wise giants. Just as strong are our memories of them as the terrible meanies who wouldn't let us wear our hair a certain way, stay out all night, and ignore our homework. If you were to meet your friend's father today, your impression of him might be more real than your friend's because you wouldn't be bringing extra baggage into the present reality. On the other hand, you would bring your impressions about fathers in general. If your friend's father was a plumber, you would bring all your perceptions about plumbers; if he was elderly, you would superimpose your feelings about senior citizens; and so on. You would see the past in him, but in a different way from your friend.

We have similar reactions to all kinds of mundane events. Imagine a child being reared in a poor family. For him, the daily arrival of the mail is an unhappy time, for it brings notices from bill collectors that upset his parents terribly. Think of another child who loves the mail because it brings Dad's frequent bonus checks and invitations to friends' birthday parties. Now that the two children are grown-up, the first has a vaguely nervous reaction to the arrival of the mail, while the other waits for it with happy anticipation. Their feelings have nothing to do with the content of their mail today; they see the mail in the past.

We tend not to know who others are today—and the same holds true for ourselves. We generally see ourselves as we were, or as we want to be, rather than as who we really are.

There is a wonderful freedom in knowing that who we were yesterday does not absolutely define who we are now. You need not be chained to your past. Many of us wake up every morning and shower, washing off yesterday's dirt, yet still carrying yesterday's emotional stuff. It doesn't have to be that way. We can become new and begin anew, we can greet the day fresh and clean—*if* we can focus our awareness on the present, *if* we can see life as it really is. When we're not living in the moment, we don't really see each other or ourselves. And if we're not living in the moment, we can't find happiness. We shouldn't shut the door on the past, but we do need to see it for what it was and move on. Hopefully, we'll move into the now, the present, the moment we actually live in.

Jack had the ability to always be in the present moment. A runner who had raced in several marathons, he always seemed to be fully present. When he walked into a room, he looked around as if it were brand-new, even if he had been there a thousand times before. When he greeted you and asked how you were, he was paying attention. When he talked with you, he really listened—he wasn't thinking about what he was having for lunch, his date that night, or how much memory he was going to add to his computer. Jack was always there, tangibly in the present, with you and for you.

Unfortunately, Jack came down with a type of lymphoma that was particularly cruel to him because it affected his legs, causing them to swell and to be the first part of his body to go. But his quality of being in the present moment became even more marked as he got sicker. When you visited Jack and asked him how he was, you could almost see him making a survey of his mind and body to see how he was doing. In the same way, when he asked how you were, he was still so in the moment you felt incredibly connected to him as he listened to what was going on with you. He was an eloquent example of being fully present in life. Not only did he not get stuck in his distant past, but once he moved on to you, he was done with what he had just said about himself. He knew how to live in the moment and invited you to do the same. You couldn't give him pat answers to questions such as "How are you?" and "What's new?" He made you really want to look at yourself and respond fully. He never wanted to miss a moment, he didn't want to miss a thing. Jack was never in fall, still experiencing summer. He was never in winter, distracted by hopes of spring. He was fully present in every season of his life.

After meeting someone like Jack, you begin to understand how this moment can be robbed by your past and future. You have no idea what a better experience you would have if you let go of the past, at this moment, to focus on this moment, to fully experience it and really live your life. While talking to your spouse, fully engage in the conversation instead of thinking about the class you're going to teach tonight. Afterward, go prepare for your class. You'll have a better experience with your spouse and will make a better presentation in class. Take one moment at a time.

We have come to rely on our futures. Some live in the

future, some dream about it, and some dread it. All these approaches keep us out of the moment. One man in his fifties, who had finally had to leave work because of illness, woke up in the middle of the night in a panic. He opened his appointment book only to see week after week after week of empty pages. His future seemed literally to be a blank. He said he knew in dealing with this illness that he would have to let go of the past. He knew he would also have to let go of the future, but not until he opened his appointment book so frantically that night did he see what letting go of the future looks like. He had to let go of the structure of time we live and get lost in. Through this loss, he began to learn who he was and about his relationship with time. At first, he had to grapple with the reality that time, as he knew it, was beginning to break down. For example, when friends called to ask what time they should visit, he said any time was good, it didn't matter. Through this he began to get a sense that he is continuing even though time—and filling it as he used to—is breaking down. When he searched deeper, he realized that when time is no more, he will continue. "The more artificial time began to break down," he explained, "the more I realized I lived in time and will die in time. And I began to feel, innately, how I am eternal and will exist past time. I will continue. At our core, we are actually timeless."

The reality of time is that we can't be certain about the past. We don't know if it really happened the way we think it did. And certainly we don't know the future. In fact, we don't even know for sure if time is linear.

We think of the past as coming *before* and the future as lying *ahead,* but that assumes time lies on a straight-line continuum. Scientists have speculated that time is not linear, that we are not locked into a rigid past-present-future pattern. In nonlinear time, the past, present, and future may all exist at the same time.

Does this possibility matter? Will our lives be changed if time is not linear, if we are simultaneously in the past, present, and future?

✤ D K

Frank and Margaret had been married for over fifty wonderful years. Devotedly in love with each other, they were inseparable. When Margaret became terminally ill, she said, "I can accept this illness. I can accept that I'm going to die. The hardest thing for me to accept is that I'm going to be without Frank."

As Margaret's disease progressed, she was more and more disturbed by the prospect of this ultimate separation. Hours before she died, she turned to Frank, who was sitting at her bedside. Her mind was clear and alert, for she had not taken any medications. She said, "I'm going to be leaving soon. And it's finally okay."

"What has made it okay for you?" he asked.

"I've just been told I'm going to a place where you already are. You will be there when I get there."

Is it possible that Frank is simultaneously sitting in the hospital room and waiting for his beloved wife in heaven? Perhaps. Or perhaps the questions revolve around our perception of time. For Frank, who lives and breathes in time, it may be five, ten, or twenty years before he sees Margaret again. But if she is going to a place where there is no more time, it may seem that he arrives a second behind her. Time is longer for the survivor than for the one who dies.

✤ ✤ ✤

When a doctor tells people that they have a terminal illness, their feelings about time become intense. Suddenly they fear there's not enough of it. Here's another of life's contradictions: moving from abstract to real, you see your time as limited for the first time. But does any doctor really know when someone has six months? No matter what we know about the average length of survival, you cannot know when you will die. You have to grapple with the reality of not knowing. Sometimes the lesson becomes clear. Standing at the edge of life, you want to know how much time you have left, but you realize that you have never known. In looking at the lives and deaths of others we often say that people died before their time. We feel their lives were incomplete, but there are only two requirements for a complete life: birth and death. In fact, we rarely pronounce a life complete unless the person lived to be ninety-five years old and had a great life. Otherwise, we proclaim the death premature.

Beethoven was "only" fifty-seven when he died, yet his accomplishments were tremendous. Joan of Arc was not even twenty when her life was taken, yet she is remembered and venerated today. John F. Kennedy Jr. died with his wife and sister-in-law at age thirty-eight. He never held an elected office, yet he was more loved than many of our presidents. Were any of these lives incomplete? This question takes us back to the wristwatch concept of life, by which everything is measured and judged artificially. But we don't know what lessons others are supposed to learn, we don't know who they were supposed to be or how much time they were supposed to have. As hard as it may be to accept, the reality is that we don't die before our time. When we die, it *is* our time.

Our challenge is to fully experience this moment—and it's a great challenge. To know that this instant contains all the possibilities for happiness and love and not lose these possibilities in expectations of what the future should look like. In putting aside our sense of anticipation we can live in the sacred space of what is happening now.

CHAPTER EIGHT

THE LESSON OF FEAR

✤DK

Christopher Landon, son of the late actor Michael Landon, was sixteen years old when his father died in 1991. Christopher spoke about the effect that losing his father had on him and his fears:

"As you would expect, his death had a huge impact on me. I look back with much longing. My dad was so bright and so charming and witty. There were so many sides to him—that the public didn't get to see—that made the whole person that I knew.

"His death was the most important event of my life. It changed me as a person. As a child, I was always very introverted, shy, and insecure. Growing up with someone who is bigger than life, you are always in their shadow. Then that shadow was pulled away one day.

"Noticing many of my fears fade after he died got me thinking about death in general. When you love someone and they die, you form your first relationship with death. You come close to it, you are less afraid of it because you've been with it. I was with my father when he was dying, and after he passed away. I touched death and it touched me.

It's real to me now, it's tangible. It's also less frightening. Everything is less frightening. I am not afraid of the same things I was afraid of before my father died. I used to be so afraid of flying, I was a white-knuckle flier. My dad would laugh. After he died, that fear, and many others, subsided. I wasn't conscious of it, but I started doing things completely out of character. I started being assertive and doing things I never did before.

"Before, every time I came to a crossroad, every time I had an opportunity to take a chance, to get ahead, I balked. I was afraid of failing, of looking like an idiot. So I usually ignored the opportunity.

"Then he died, and I faced death. I realized you never know when you're going to die, and that you should face every challenge with that understanding. I started feeling more comfortable in my shoes. No longer afraid of myself, of who I am and who I might be, I started to take some chances and do things. I wasn't jumping out of airplanes or anything that drastic, but I left home and went to school in England. That was a big step for me, leaving the comfort and safety of my home. I've learned how to throw myself into the mix and see what happens. That was a big step for me. I am a firm believer that somehow pain translates into growth."

What if we started taking some chances, if we stepped into our fears? What if we went further, if we were to pursue our dreams, follow our desires? And what if we allowed ourselves to experience love freely and to find fulfillment in our relationships? What kind of world would this be? A world without fear. It may be hard to believe, but there is so much more to life than we let ourselves experience. So much more is possible when fear no longer holds us captive. There is a new world outside of us and inside of us—one where there is less fear—just waiting to be discovered.

Fear is a warning system that, on a primal level, serves us well. If we're walking late at night in a dangerous part of town, fear warns us to be on guard against the genuine possibility of trouble. In potentially dangerous situations, fear is a sign of health. It is a protector. Without it we would not survive long.

But it's easy to experience fear where there is no danger. That kind of fear is made up, it's not real. The feeling may seem real, but it has no basis in reality. Still, it keeps us up at night, it keeps us from living. It seems to have no purpose and no mercy, it paralyzes us and weakens the spirit when left unattended. It's summed up by the acronym FEAR, which stands for False Evidence Appearing Real. This type of fear is based in the past and triggers fear of the future. These invented fears do serve a purpose: They give us the opportunity to learn to choose love. They are cries from our soul for growth, for healing. They are opportunities to choose again. To do it differently, to choose love over fear, reality over illusion, now over the past. For the purposes of this chapter, and our happiness, when we refer to fear we're talking about these invented fears that make our lives less worth living.

If we can find our way through our fears, if we can take advantage of so many opportunities, we can live the lives we've only dreamed about. We can live free of judgment, without fearing the disapproval of others, without holding back.

❖ E K R

Kate, an energetic woman in her midfifties, spoke of her twin sister, Kim. "Ten years ago, Kim found out she had colon cancer. Luckily it was not very aggressive and was diagnosed early. Besides making me feel like part of me would die if she died, Kim's disease—and her life—really shook me up. Being identical twins, we not only knew all the facts about each other's life, we also knew each other's emotions. And I can see how fear stopped her and me from living long before the cancer came along. I now look back at our lives and see how much fear we had.

"When we were in Hawaii, we wanted to learn to hula dance, but were afraid we'd look foolish. For ten years we worked for a catering company. We always wanted to open our own restaurant but were afraid we wouldn't make it, so we never even explored the idea. After my divorce we were thinking about going on a cruise. But we didn't go because we were afraid to go on our own.

"Now our lives are completely different. We always thought we had something to fear. After we dealt with Kim's illness and her surgery, we had gone through our greatest fear. If we survived that, what else was there to fear? I understand now that most of what we fear isn't going to happen anyway. Our fears are usually not related to what really happens to us."

❖ ❖ ❖

Much of what life hands us comes without the prelude of fear and worry. Our fears don't stop death, they stop life. More than we care to admit, more than we even know, our lives are devoted to dealing with fear and its effects. Fear is a shadow that blocks everything: our love, our true feelings, our happiness, our very being.

A child grew up in a foster home facility under the care of a couple who were abusive. The boy finally heard that he would be going to a wonderful new home with parents who would love him. He would live in a nice home, have his own room and even a TV, but he cried in fear. He knew the situation he lived in; as bad as it was, it had become familiar. The new home, on the other hand, was full of unknown dangers. He had lived in fear so long he could not see a future without it.

We are all like this child. Raised in fear, we see only fear in the future. Our culture sells fear. Watch the little commercials that tell you what will be on the local evening news: "Why the food you're eating may be dangerous!" "Why the clothes your child is wearing may not be safe." "Why your vacation this year could kill you—a special report at six."

But how much of what we fear is going to happen? The truth is, there really isn't a big correlation between what we fear and what happens to us. The reality is that the food we eat is safe, our children's clothes will not suddenly catch fire, and our vacations will be fun.

Still, our lives are often governed by fear. Insurance companies bet us that most of what we worry about will never happen. And they win, to the tune of billions of dollars each year. The point is not that we shouldn't have insurance. The point is this: Odds are, we will have great fun participating in challenging sports. The chances are good we will survive and possibly even thrive in the business world, despite taking a few risks and occasionally stumbling. And we'll have fun and meet lots of nice people at social gatherings. Yet most of us live our lives as if the odds are stacked against us. One of our biggest challenges here is to try to overcome these fears. We are presented with so many opportunities and we need to learn to make the most of them.

✤DK

Troy, who had been living with AIDS for three years, considered himself lucky because he had never been sick from the disease. Physically Troy was doing well, but mentally he was paralyzed by fear. He was used to garden-variety fear, having lived with it most of his life. "It had never been paralyzing," he explained, "just bad enough to make me keep a distance from life. Now, with AIDS, I was devastated. It was like all my fears had consolidated themselves into one big disease.

"My partner, Vincent, is always supportive. He keeps telling me that I am stronger than my fears. Just step forward, he says, face them. Take your worst fear to lunch and you'll find it doesn't have the power over you that you think it does.

"I thought, 'Face my fears, take them to lunch, step forward? Isn't it enough that I'm living with AIDS?' The truth is I would much rather take issue with what he said than look at it. No one knew more than me how much my fears ate me up alive.

"I was between jobs when one of Vincent's coworkers approached me. He told me his sister, Jackie, had AIDS and had just been released from the hospital. They were having a hard time getting anyone to help her and wondered if I would. I told him I would think about it and call him back. Then I went to Vincent for his advice. He said, 'She desperately needs the help and you could use the money.' I asked him how sick she was and he said he thought she was dying.

"When he said that, every fear I had rose up within me. I asked, 'Does everyone think I am uniquely qualified to take care of her because I am dying?'

"'No,' Vincent said. 'They are hoping you might not be afraid of the disease because you have it.'

"'Boy,' I thought, 'did they ever get the wrong person.'

"I couldn't commit to it, I was too afraid. Vincent reminded me that I didn't have to do it if I didn't want to, but he thought I should meet her. I was afraid to. Then I thought I had been afraid long enough, so I decided to step forward and meet her.

"I asked Vincent to go with me to her house. I walked up to her door, turned around, and said, 'Vincent, I'm sorry, I can't do it.'

"He said, 'Okay, let's go home and call them.'

"But I looked at her door again. There, right through the door, were all my fears. I decided to walk into them and just see what happens. Something made me go through the door.

"Inside, I looked at her sitting in a wheelchair. She must have weighed eighty pounds. She had suffered a double stroke, so she couldn't speak very well. She had the biggest brown eyes I had ever seen. I looked into them and saw all this fear there. It was written on her forehead: 'I am afraid I am dying, I am afraid I will die alone, I am afraid no one will be there for me, I am afraid you will leave.' There were my biggest fears sitting right in front of me! I looked at her and was so sad. I just kept hearing in my mind, 'Step forward. Just step into your fear.' I closed my eyes and asked, 'Can I start today?'

"I knew I needed to help her, this stranger I didn't know. Later, I found out that her parents wanted nothing to do with her now that she had AIDS. They wanted to pay someone to deal with it. They were just waiting for her to die. She had a couple of friends who came over, but not that often. I went from helping part-time, to working full-time, to being her best friend. I didn't expect to move through my fears, yet I did. I came to love her.

"Toward the end she was hospitalized again. She wanted me there because she was so frightened. On her last day, I went in. The hospital had called her parents, but they stayed in the waiting room. I sat with her, looking at those big brown eyes. I told her I was with her. I could feel her fear. I had never felt anything so intense. Then it popped into my head again: 'Step forward, it has no power.' I told her, 'I am holding your hand. I am going to stay here and hold your hand until they take you on the other side. Then, they will hold your hand. No fears, Jackie, no fears.'

"Then she died. I watched her chest stop moving up and down.

"The mortuary came to pick her up: they were upset that no one had told them she had AIDS, and they were afraid to touch her. So a nurse and I volunteered to put Jackie in the body bag. I was tired of feeling fear around her. I thought, 'No more.' I would rather do it myself than let them near her. It was the hardest thing I had ever done in my life. I just kept saying to her, 'No fears, Jackie, no fears."

Troy fought fear with love, and won. Kindness always overcomes fear. That's how you beat it; it is no match for love. Fear's power is built on an empty foundation, it can be defeated just by stepping forward.

❖ ❖ ❖

We're afraid of many things in life, such as public speaking, dating, and even admitting we're lonely sometimes. In many cases it's easier not to try rather than to be rejected and deal with the feelings underneath. Indeed, fears are tricky because they are so well layered, one on top of the other. Each can be peeled away until you get down to the bottom fear, the foundation on which all the others rest. And that's usually the fear of death.

Suppose you're extremely worried about a project at work. Peel away that fear and underneath you'll find the fear of not doing well. Underneath that you'll find successive layers: fear of not getting the raise, of losing your job, and then finally fear of not surviving, which is essentially the fear of death. The fear of not surviving underlies many of our financial and job-related fears.

Suppose you're afraid to ask someone out on a date. Beneath that fear is the fear of rejection, and underneath that is the fear that there won't be someone for you. Underneath that is the fear that you're unlovable, and if you're not loved, can you possibly survive? When people have inadequacies, the bottom-line fear is "I'm not enough." Why do people stand in corners at parties not talking to anyone? Because they fear they're not good at meeting and talking to others at parties, which means they fear they're not enough. *Other people* are charming enough, *other people* are pretty enough, sweet enough, interesting enough, but these people fear they are not.

It all boils down to the fear of death, arguably the cause of most of our unhappiness. We unknowingly harm our loved ones out of fear; we hold ourselves back personally and professionally for the same reason. Since every fear has its roots in the fear of death, learning to relax about the fear surrounding death will allow us to face everything else with greater ease.

The dying are facing that ultimate fear, the fear of death. They are facing that fear and they realize that it does not crush them, that it has no more power over them. The dying have learned that fear doesn't matter; but for the rest of us, it is still very real.

If we could literally reach into you and remove all your fears—every one of them—how different would your life be? Think about it. If nothing stopped you from following your dreams, your life would probably be very different. This is what the dying learn. Dying makes our worst fears come forward to be faced directly. It helps us see the different life that is possible and, in that vision, takes the rest of our fears away.

Unfortunately, by the time the fear is gone most of us are too sick or too old to do those things we would have done before, had we not been afraid. We become old and ill without ever trying our secret passions, finding our true work, or becoming the people we'd like to be. If we did the things we're longing to do, we would still be old and ill one day—but we would not be filled with regrets. We would not be ending a life half-lived. Thus, one lesson becomes clear: we must transcend our fears while we can still do those things we dream of.

To transcend fear, though, we must move somewhere else emotionally; we must move into love.

Happiness, anxiety, joy, resentment—we have many words for the many emotions we experience in our lifetimes. But deep down, at our cores, there are only two emotions: love and fear. All positive emotions come from love, all negative emotions from fear. From love flows happiness, contentment, peace, and joy. From fear comes anger, hate, anxiety, and guilt.

It's true that there are only two primary emotions, love and fear, but it's more accurate to say that there is only love *or* fear, for we cannot feel these two emotions together, at exactly the same time. They're opposites. If we're in fear, we're not in a place of love. When we're in a place of love, we cannot be in a place of fear. Can you think of a time when you've been in both love and fear? It's impossible.

We have to make a decision to be in one place or the other; there is no neutrality in this. If you don't actively choose love, you will find yourself in a place of either fear or one of its component feelings. Every moment offers the choice to choose one or the other. And we must continually make these choices, especially in difficult circumstances when our commitment to love, instead of fear, is challenged.

Having chosen love doesn't mean you will never fear again. In fact, it means many of your fears will come up to finally be healed. This is an ongoing process. Remember that you will become fearful after you've chosen love, just as we become hungry after we eat. We must continually choose love in order to nourish our souls and drive away fear, just as we eat to nourish our bodies and drive away hunger. Just like Troy caring for Jackie; he continually chose kindness over fear. He decided to serve something greater than his fear; he chose to serve another human being in need. It doesn't mean his fear won't come up again. Whenever his fear returns, he will have to return to love in the present moment.

All of our invented fears involve either the past or the future; only love is in the present. *Now* is the only real moment we have, and love is the only real emotion because it's the only one that occurs in the present moment. Fear is always based on something that happened in the past and causes us to be afraid of something we think may happen in the future. To live in the present, then, is to live in love, not fear. That's our goal, to live in love. And we can work toward that goal by learning to love ourselves. Infusing ourselves with love begins the washing away of our fears.

✤ EKR

Unfortunately, many of us are filled with fear. Many of us are like Joshua, a thirty-five-year-old graphic artist who freelances for printers. He had studied art and dreamed of painting, but now spends most of his time designing business cards.

This young man had great plans once, but was afraid to reach for the brass ring. "It's just the way I am," he insisted. "I'm just not the type of guy who succeeds."

As we discussed this, I tried to figure out what made him feel so unworthy. It wasn't that he had suffered a tremendous failure or humiliation; he couldn't have, because he hasn't painted anything since college. Back and forth we went until we stumbled into talking about the death of his father. "My father was like me," Joshua explained. "He wanted to do a lot of things, but just couldn't get 'em done. He's like me, a sort of failure."

As we continued talking, we realized that there was no obvious reason for his father's inability to live his dreams.

"Why was your father a 'sort of failure'?" I persisted in asking. "Was he dumb? Unable to get along with people? Untalented? Did he have a long history of failure? What held him back?"

Joshua thought for a long, long time before finally saying, "There was nothing wrong with him. He was smart, he was talented, and he got along with people. He could have done whatever he wanted, but he never tried. And he was always saying, 'Things never work out for people in our family.' I even remember how, when Dad was dying, he wanted to contact an old childhood friend, whom he hadn't seen in twenty years. But he didn't, because he thought the guy wouldn't want to hear from him after such a long time."

Joshua suddenly looked stricken. He continued, "I know what he was talking about. I always feel like I'm not good enough. Not good enough to paint."

The problem for this young man wasn't that he was designing business cards instead of painting, it was that he felt inadequate, not good enough to take a chance pursuing his profession fully. I asked him what he would do differently right now if he wasn't afraid. He replied, "I would take a painting class."

That would be a case of not letting fear get in the way. "That would be different from your father, wouldn't it?" I asked.

He thought for a moment, then answered, "Yes. Dad died with all his fears in place."

Joshua has the opportunity for a different life, a life with less fear. Maybe he will be a great painter, or maybe he will simply enjoy painting for its own sake. Either way, he will not live a life of fear, or die with one.

❖ ❖ ❖

We all live with the possibility of death, but the dying live with the probability. What do they do with that heightened awareness? They take more risks, because they haven't anything to lose anymore. Patients at the edge of life will tell you that they find incredible happiness in realizing that there is nothing to fear, nothing to lose. It is fear itself that brings us so much unhappiness in life, not the things we fear. Fear wears many disguises—anger, protection, self-sufficiency. We must turn our fear into wisdom. Step forward a little every day. Practice doing the small things that you are afraid of doing. Your fear only holds enormous power over you when not challenged. Learn to use the power of love and kindness to overcome fear.

Compassion can help you harness your love and kindness when you're faced with fear. The next time you're afraid, have compassion.

If you are around someone who is sick, even with something minor such as a cold, you may want to distance yourself because you're afraid you'll catch it. Instead, have compassion—you know what it's like to have a cold.

If you are stopped because you're afraid that you or what you've done isn't good enough, have compassion for yourself. Suppose you've prepared a report on your great new idea but are afraid to show it to your boss. You might be thinking, "I'm afraid she'll hate the report, I'm not good enough, I'll get fired." If you give your attention to these fears, they grow and expand. But suppose you had compassion for yourself. Suppose you acknowledged that you're doing the best you can and that you prepared the report with care, which is all that matters. If your mind goes to your boss's reaction, have compassion for her knowing that she just wants to do her job well and is doing the best she can. If you do that, you'll be introducing compassion and love to dissipate your fear. You will be surprised how compassion melts away fear.

If you're afraid to speak to people at social or business gatherings because you don't know them, remember that most of the other people are in the same situation. They don't know everyone present, they're afraid no one will want to speak to them, some of them would rather sneak out and go home. Remind yourself that they would like to be treated with compassion, just as you would. Having compassion for them takes you out of your fear. You'll find you're able to approach people more easily if you have compassion for them, as well as for yourself.

If we can understand that everyone else is a little frightened on the inside, just as we are, we can begin to live with more compassion and less fear. Inside the boss or the sick person or the partygoers are people who have fears, just as you do, and deserve compassion, just as you do.

If you live in fear, you are not really living. Any thought you have either reinforces your fear or enlarges your love. Love grows more love, it expands itself. Fear grows more fear, especially when it is hidden. You also create more fear when you act from fear.

True freedom is found in doing the things that scare us the most. Take a leap and you will find life, not lose it. Sometimes living a safe life, with lots of respect for all our fears, worries, and anxieties, is the most dangerous thing we can do. Don't make fear a permanent part of your life: letting go, or at least living in spite of fear, surprisingly and paradoxically, returns you to a place of safety. You can learn to love without hesitation, to speak without caution, and to care without self-defensiveness.

Once we are on the other side of our fears, we find new life. Ultimately, love becomes letting go of our fears. As Helen Keller said, "Life is either a daring adventure or it's nothing." If we can learn these lessons of fear, we can lead a life of awe and wonder. A life beyond our dreams, without fear.

CHAPTER NINE

THE LESSON OF ANGER

A nurse at a Midwest hospital emergency room got a call from the dispatcher informing her that five people in critical condition were being brought in. The situation, already tense, was complicated because one of the injured was the nurse's husband. The other four were a family she didn't know. Despite the doctors' and nurses' best efforts, all five died.

What killed them? A building collapse? A bus crash? A drive-by shooting? A fire?

Anger killed them.

One car had been trying to pass another on a rural road. But each driver refused to yield. Side by side they raced ahead, jockeying for position, fueled by anger. Neither one saw the third car heading toward them until it was too late.

The nurse's husband was one of those angry drivers.

The two men trying to pass each other were strangers—they had never even met. They had no reason to be this angry with each other, yet they were overcome with rage simply because one wanted to pass the other. Charges were filed against the surviving driver.

Three families were devastated by this tragic accident

resulting from anger, which some officials believe is the number one cause of auto accidents in our country today.

We can all identify with driving while angry, but luckily, few of us suffer such extreme consequences. Yet, letting anger build up as these two men did can be a substantial negative force in our lives. We must learn to express it in healthy ways so that we can control it before it controls us.

Anger is a natural emotion, which, in its natural state, should only take a few seconds to a few minutes to externalize. For example, if someone cuts in front of us in line at the movies, it's only natural for us to be angry at him or her for about a minute. If we naturally felt our anger by expressing it—if we let it live for a minute in order to move through it—we would be fine. But problems arise when we either express anger inappropriately by blowing up or suppress it so that it accumulates. We end up either giving a situation more of our anger than it deserves, or none of it.

Suppressed anger does not simply evaporate, it becomes unfinished business. If we don't deal with that little bit of anger, it gets bigger and bigger until it has to go someplace, usually the wrong place. Those two drivers were so full of old anger that, when they encountered each other, it exploded. In no more than a few seconds, they blew up like volcanoes.

The other problem with accumulating anger is that even if the people who hurt us are willing to take responsibility for their actions, it isn't enough. If they apologize and we believe the apology was sincere yet continue to be angry, that is old anger. And it can rise to the surface over and over again, in different and unexpected ways.

Many people were raised in families where showing any anger was wrong. Others came from families where even the slightest problem escalated to rage. It is no wonder we have no good role models for expressing this natural emotion. Instead of understanding what to do with anger, we question it, wonder if it is valid, misplace it, and do just about everything we can—except feel it. But anger is a normal reaction, useful at the right time and place, and in the proper portions. For example, studies have shown over and over again that angry patients live longer. Whether that's because they externalize their feelings or because they demand better care, we don't know. We do know that anger creates action and helps us control the world around us. It also helps us set appropriate boundaries in our lives. As long as it's not inappropriate, violent, or abusive, anger can be a helpful and healthy response.

As one of the body's important warning systems, anger should not automatically be stifled. It warns us that we are being hurt or our needs are not being heard; it can be a normal and healthy reaction to many situations. On the other hand, it may, like guilt, be a signal that something is out of line with our belief systems. Occasional anger, registered in proportion to harmful events, is healthy—it's what we sometimes do or do not do with the feeling that causes problems. Often we are so afraid of our own anger and deny it so deeply, we are no longer aware of it.

Anger doesn't have to be a horrible beast that consumes our lives. It's just a feeling. It isn't productive to overanalyze it or to ask if it is valid, appropriate, or warranted. To do so is to wonder if we should even have feelings. Anger is just that—a feeling. It's a feeling to be experienced, not judged. Like all our feelings, anger is a form of communication, it brings us a message.

Unfortunately, many of us no longer hear its message. We often don't know how to feel it. When people in anger are asked "What are you feeling?" they will begin to answer by saying, "I think . . ." That is an intellectual answer to an emotional question. It comes from our minds, not from our guts.

We must get in touch with the feelings in our bellies. Sometimes people find this so difficult that it's helpful for them to close their eyes and put one hand on their stomach. This simple motion helps them get in touch with what they are feeling, probably because it uses the body, not just the brain. Getting in touch with our feelings is almost a foreign notion in our society: we forget that we feel with our bodies. We tend to split our minds from our emotions. We're so used to letting our minds dominate that we forget our feelings and our bodies. Notice how many times you begin a sentence with "I think" rather than "I feel."

Anger tells us that we haven't dealt with our hurt. Hurt is present pain, while anger is often lingering pain. As we gather these hurts and do not address them, our anger grows. We can accumulate many hurts, and it becomes hard to sort them out—eventually, even hard to recognize the anger. We get so used to living with the feeling that we begin to think of it as part of who we are. We begin to see ourselves as bad people. The anger becomes part of our identity. We must begin the task of separating our old feelings from our identity. We must release this anger to remember our good and remember who we are.

Besides becoming angry with others, we become angry with ourselves, mad at what we did or didn't do. We become angry because we feel we've betrayed ourselves, often in trying to please others at the expense of our feelings. We get angry when we fail to honor our own needs and wants. We know we're mad at "them" for not giving us what we deserve, but we don't always realize that we're angry with ourselves for not giving to ourselves first. Sometimes we're just too stubborn to admit that we have needs, because in our society, need equals weakness.

When we turn our anger inward, it often expresses itself in feelings of depression or guilt. Anger held internally changes our impressions of the past and distorts our view of current reality. All of this old anger becomes unfinished business not merely with others, but with ourselves.

We tend to bounce from one extreme to another, holding our anger in and "letting it blow," blaming others and blaming ourselves. We're not letting anger express itself naturally, so it's no wonder we think it's bad. It's no wonder we think people who yell are ill-tempered, but just because we're not yelling, too, doesn't mean we are at peace or free from anger.

❖ D K

Berry Berenson Perkins, wife of the late actor Anthony Perkins, is one of the most charming women you will ever meet. Her mixture of grace, style, and warmth puts you instantly at ease. Yet, under this soft veneer lies a great deal of pain. Fortunately, she has had the courage to confront the anger that lives beneath the surface. She hadn't spoken about this publicly, but when I told her I was writing another book, she said, "I want to share this because I think it can help others."

She notes, "Everybody deals with grief in different ways. The most important thing is to talk about it and find ways to get your anger out. So many people say 'Get over it already' or 'Deal with the anger,' but they haven't experienced what you have. As someone who has gone through it, I can tell you that it is one of the toughest things you will ever do.

"I had to come to grips with the reality that I was angry a lot of the time. Angry that there was not someone there to help me to finish raising the kids. Angry that I had to cope on my own when I used to have someone else to cope with me. I see now I was angry with Tony for leaving us. It's an underlying anger. I found myself angry and I didn't know why.

"I realized I took it out on the dishes or myself. I hope to get it out completely one day. I think the more one deals with one's anger, the more one gets it out. I've written him letters and done a lot of work to bring out the anger and direct it.

"It is also important to bring out the good feelings you have for that person so that you can balance the anger and not feel angry all the time. After his death we were shocked and confused. We repressed our anger, which turned into depression. I just loved him so much and I didn't want to blame him for anything, but you can't help it.

"I have learned so many lessons about anger. I learned that I was never in touch with my anger. Most married couples experience anger from time to time. We never had angry arguments, we avoided them as a family. We never wanted to say mean things that might hurt the other person. We were very nice to one another. We skirted a lot of anger issues. But it's hard to forgive if you haven't dealt with the anger. The more anger you can let go of, the more forgiveness you are going to have."

❖ ❖ ❖

Untreated fear turns into anger. When we're not in touch with our fears—or when we don't even know we're afraid—that fear grows into anger. If we don't deal with the anger, it will turn into rage.

We're more accustomed to dealing with our anger than with our fear. It's easier for us to say to a spouse "I'm angry at you" than it is to say "I'm afraid you'll leave." It's easier to get angry about what's going wrong than to admit "I am afraid I'm not good enough."

A young man named Andrew was supposed to meet his girlfriend, Melanie, at a coffeehouse a few months ago. But several of these coffeehouses are spread throughout the city, and each went to a different one. Andrew waited for Melanie for thirty or forty minutes, left a message on her answering machine, and went back to his apartment. "I figured that there must have been some sort of mix-up, so we'd try again," he explained. "That was not Melanie's impression. She was very angry with me. She was implying that I deliberately left her there, that I disappointed her, that I couldn't be trusted. I pointed out that we both just assumed it was a different coffeehouse."

What for Andrew was a simple mix-up was for Melanie a horrible letdown suggesting he was unreliable and would disappoint her again. She brought more anger to the situation than it deserved, anger that was possibly left over from an old hurt. She couldn't see reality as it was.

Out of touch with the fear under her anger, Melanie made Andrew the villain. Unfortunately, she only took the first step—she got mad. We're all very good at this step: "I'm angry because you weren't there," "I'm angry because you were late," "I'm angry because you didn't do a good job," "I'm angry because of what you said." We need to learn how to take the second step, looking into ourselves to explore the fear underneath. Here are some clues to what may really be going on:

- The anger: I'm angry because you weren't there.
- The fear underneath: When you're not there, I fear you're abandoning me.

- The anger: I'm angry because you're late.
- The fear underneath: I'm not as important to you as your work.

- The anger: I'm angry because you didn't do a good job.
- The fear underneath: I'm afraid we'll make less money and not be able to pay our bills.

- The anger: I'm angry because of what you said.
- The fear underneath: I'm afraid you don't love me anymore.

It's easier to keep rubbing in the anger than it is to deal with the fear, but it doesn't help solve the underlying problem. In fact, it often only makes the "surface" problem worse, for people don't respond well to anger. Yelling at people rarely convinces them that they are wrong. Have you ever heard someone say, "They yelled at me for ten minutes, but I still thought I was right. But during the next twenty minutes of yelling I really understood their point."

Even when we have valid fears, they can be made invalid by too much anger. For instance, constantly reminding a coworker that she's late does not help the situation. But if you say, "There's so much to do, I'm afraid we're not going to get it done," she can relate to your fear without feeling wronged by your anger.

It takes a lot of energy to hold anger in, yet we all carry pain that darkens our souls. Daphne Rose Kingma, a therapist and author, held a workshop for those who were dealing with the end of a relationship. She said, "I will always remember this remarkable, poignant woman. She was in her late seventies. I thought, 'What is this woman doing here? Is she ending a relationship?' We went around the room and everybody told their story: why I am here, who left me on Christmas Day, what I am trying to get over, how it ended, can you believe it! And finally I came to this woman and I said, 'What are you doing here, are you ending a relationship?' She replied, 'I ended a relationship forty years ago with my husband, and I was so bitter and angry that I have spent these forty years *being* bitter and angry. I have complained to my children about my ex-husband, I've complained to everybody I know. I've never trusted another man. I have never been in another relationship for more than three weeks before some issue came up that reminded me of that dastardly man I was married to. I have never been able to get over it. And now I am dying, I am terminally ill with only a few months to live. I don't want to take all this anger to my grave. I am so, so sad that I lived all this life without ever loving again. So that is why I am here. I couldn't live in peace, but I do want to die in peace.'

"If you wonder if you have the courage or the strength, if you wonder if you are ever going to get over that anger, remember this woman, she is a great and tragic teacher."

Our society feels that anger is bad and wrong, so we don't have healthy ways to externalize it. We're not familiar with how to talk about it or let it out. We stuff it, deny it, or contain it. Most of us hold it inside until we finally blow because we've never learned to say, "I'm angry about the small things." Most people don't know how to stay current and say, "I'm angry about this," and when something happens tomorrow, to say, "I'm angry at that." Instead, they know how to pretend to be nice people who never get angry until they blow up and list the twenty things the other person did in the last few months that have made them angry.

Dying produces an enormous amount of anger on everyone's part. Where does the hospital staff take its anger? Where do families and patients take their anger? It would be great if hospitals had a room where you could go and scream—not at anyone, just out loud. Wouldn't it be great if we all had a safe room where we could let out our anger? Because if you don't let your anger out, you will scream at someone. And screaming at someone carries its own set of consequences. No one enjoys being around an angry person. An angry person is often a lonely person.

Many hold anger in sometimes because they judge it. They believe that if they were good people, if they were loving and spiritual, they wouldn't and shouldn't be angry. Yet, this anger may be a normal reaction. It's important to help people work through any feelings of anger they have toward themselves or other people, or even toward God.

It helps some people to call God names, scream into a pillow, even pound a baseball bat on their hospital beds to externalize their anger. They will often afterwards talk about how good it feels to have finally let that anger out. And they realize that they were afraid if they ever spoke those words, their God would strike them with lightning or otherwise punish them, but now they feel closer to God than ever. As one woman said, "I realized my God was big enough to handle my anger. And I realized that my anger was not even about Him, anyway."

A flight attendant shared the story of her father being accidentally killed while he was cleaning his gun. She had tried and tried to make peace with his death but could not accept it. She couldn't get over it until one day at home, while thinking about his death, a terrible rain and thunderstorm began. She ran into the backyard and, in all the noise and rain, screamed at the top of her lungs into the thunder and sky about how angry she was. She said that something about that storm helped her get in touch with and express her anger. After a few minutes of screaming and raising her fist to the sky, she dropped on her knees and cried. Then, for the first time in years, she said, "I finally felt at peace again."

❖ EKR

After my strokes, I could live with the idea of dying and I could live with the idea of recovery. Instead, I had to live with being incapacitated, with my left side paralyzed, not getting better or worse. I was like a plane sitting on a runway: I wished it would either take off or go back to the gate. There was nothing to do but sit. I became angry. I was filled with anger at everything and everyone. I was even angry at God; I called him every name in the book—and lightning didn't strike me. Through the years, so many people have told me how much they appreciate my stages on death and dying, of which anger is one. But now, so many people in my life disappeared when I became angry myself. At least 75 percent of my friends left. Even some in the press condemned me for not having a "good" death because of my anger. It's as if they loved my stages but didn't like me being in one of them. But those who stayed with me allowed me to be, not judging me or my anger, and that helped to dissipate it.

I have taught that patients must be allowed to express their anger and must give themselves permission to do so.

While I was in the hospital after my first stroke, a nurse sat on my elbow. As I cried out with pain, I gave my first "karate chop." I didn't really hit her, I just made the motion with my other arm. As a result, they wrote in my chart that I was combative. This is so typical in the medical world; we overlabel patients for having normal reactions.

We are here to heal and move through feelings. Babies and young children feel their feelings and move through them. They cry and it passes, they get angry and it passes. With their honesty, the dying often begin to resemble the young children they once were. The dying remember to say "I am scared" and "I am mad." Like them, we can learn to be more honest and to express our anger. We can learn to live lives where anger is a feeling that passes, not a state of being.

CHAPTER TEN

THE LESSON OF PLAY

✣DK

One day I visited seventy-nine-year-old Lorraine at the hospital. She had just been diagnosed with lymphoma. With white hair and bracelets, she was sitting up in bed talking with her family.

Despite the grim outlook, I remember feeling that I was intruding on a happy family gathering. I introduced myself and asked if I could come back another time, when she wasn't as busy. "Sure, I love visitors," she said with a smile. As I left, I wondered if she knew exactly why I was visiting her. But she was very aware of what was going on: she was dealing with cancer.

When I came back the next day, Lorraine had the radio on and was dancing in the privacy of her room with all the enthusiasm of a seventeen-year-old. As I watched her, I thought about a cliché that nonetheless seemed so true in this moment: she was dancing as if there were no tomorrow.

Lorraine looked over as she shimmied about. I smiled and said, "Whatcha doing there?"

"The watusi."

"And why are you doing the watusi?"

"Because I can!"

She was right; we want to play because we can. Yet we also suppress the urge. Fortunately, Lorraine knew how to let herself play, even when facing serious illness.

The dying make the need for play perfectly clear. As you listen in on their conversations with loved ones, it's obvious that those moments they had shared in their leisure time, in their fun time, at play, are the moments that matter at the end of life. They'll say, "Do you remember the time we went to the beach?" and "Do you remember when we rode our bikes in the country?" They'll reminisce about "all those Sundays when we took the kids to the park" and "the funny faces Joe could make."

The answer to the question "Why is play a lesson?" can be found in deathbed regrets. The number one regret people have when they look back on their lives is "I wish I had not taken life so seriously."

In all our years of counseling patients at the edge of life, we have never had one person look at us and say, "If only I could have worked an extra day a week" or "If only there were nine work hours a day instead of eight, I would have had a happier life." People look back on their work accomplishments and other achievements with a sense of pride, but realize that there was more to life than that. They discover that if their work achievements weren't balanced by high points in their personal life, the work feels empty. They often realize that they worked hard but they didn't really live. As the saying goes, "All work and no play makes Jack a dull boy." It also makes for a dull life, one that's out of balance.

We're here to enjoy ourselves and to play—throughout life. Playing is not just a pastime for kids, it's our life force.

Playing keeps us young at heart, puts passion in our work, and helps our relationships thrive. It rejuvenates us. To play is to live life to its fullest.

Unfortunately, play is usually given a low priority. While it is true that placing a high priority on work is useful, since we all must take care of ourselves and our families, this priority has been taken too far. Too many people feel a desperate need to be constantly productive, successful, and always achieving. This generation knows how to *do,* but doesn't always know how to *be.*

The problem is usually not that someone is working eight hours a day at his or her primary job, then an additional four nights to make the mortgage and put food on the family's table. If you absolutely must work two jobs to make ends meet, then you must work the two jobs.

You may find yourself working nights and weekends not to get ahead but just because your job culture requires it. If it's temporary, it may be worth it. But if that's just going to be your life, if you're never going to have nights or weekends off, you may wonder if it's worth it.

Many people work all day and then work nights to get ahead, forgetting why they were trying to get ahead. And if they go out, it's to an event that provides good networking possibilities, rather than to a get-together that simply offers fun. Weekends are turned into "catch-up and get-ahead time" at work. When these people do attempt play on the weekends, they can't escape the nagging feeling that they're wasting their time.

To get ahead, we tend to leave the loved ones behind. We think we want to give them more. But mostly what they want is us.

Yes, success and control are important, but so is play. We

have an innate desire to play, to release, to let go, to dispel our stress and tension. Unfortunately, we have suppressed the urge to play and sometimes forgotten it's there.

Many offices will acknowledge employees' birthdays, often bringing in a cake or balloons. These balloons usually get scattered about, perhaps rising to the ceiling in the offices and hallways. If you watch workers going to the copy machine or colleagues' offices, you'll see them playing with the balloons as they pass, swatting them with their fingertips, pulling them down by their strings and watching them rise back to the ceiling, tying them around their fingers. But they will do this discreetly, when they think no one is looking.

These highly productive people are starved for play. And many people are just like them, kids without balloons. We've forgotten to play. We've forgotten how to play. We've even forgotten what play is.

We have to remind ourselves that play is doing the things that bring us pleasure, for pleasure's sake. Play is an experience of fun that transcends all boundaries. Anyone can play with others of the same or the opposite sex, of any race or religion, of any age. We can even go outside our species to play: most of us derive great joy from playing with our pets.

Playing is our inner joy, outwardly expressed. It can be laughing, singing, dancing, swimming, hiking, cooking, running, playing a game, or anything else we have fun doing.

Playing makes all aspects of life more meaningful and enjoyable. Work becomes more satisfying, our relationships improve. Play makes us feel younger, more positive. It's one of the first things children learn how to do; it's natural and instinctive.

Isn't it sad that most lives have so little pure playtime?

When people ask how they can afford to spend time playing, I answer that they can't afford *not* to. Play adds balance to our lives and improves our mental states. We work better when we have played on our time off. Whenever people tell you they are burnt-out from work, ask them what they really love doing. If they tell you they like the movies, ask, "When was the last time you saw a movie?" Usually they'll say, "A couple of months ago." To stop doing what you love is an invitation to burnout.

Playing also helps us physically. Many scientific studies have shown that laughter and play reduce stress and trigger the release of substances in the body called endorphins, which are chemically similar to morphine. These natural painkillers and mood elevators may be why we feel better after laughing and playing—they give a natural high to our lives.

Laughter is a self-refilling "medicine," for the more you laugh, the more you laugh. Even when dealing with a subject as serious as death, humor has its place.

✤EKR

An academic class on death and dying for medical and psychology students was opened to the public. The teacher, who had not thought someone who was dying would ever enroll in his class, was surprised when just that happened. Worried about the privacy of this terminally ill woman, he never shared her condition with the class. Later, he said to her, "My main concern was that someone would make a joke about dying or make light of it in some way. But this is a real matter to you, not just an intellectual exercise."

The woman replied, "Joking and playing are life. Laughing is one of the ways I get through this. If your students had made jokes, it would have been fine with me. The thing that offends me the most is when someone avoids the subject, or won't say the words *death* or *cancer*. I'd much rather joke about it, because laughter is much more fun than dread, and more real than avoidance."

❖ ❖ ❖

❖DK

Jacob Glass is an author and lecturer on spiritual principles. One afternoon I found myself chatting with this old friend at a local coffeehouse. He shared with me how he will often begin his day there, reading, enjoying his coffee, and visiting with friends. He lives not far away in a simple place that meets his needs quite well.

As we talked about his lecturing and about his writings, I found myself urging him to do more and more, explaining how he could expand his work schedule.

"And then what?" he asked.

"Then you could lecture more times per week, have the American dream, and someday retire."

"And then will I have time to sit in the coffeehouse, relax, and read?"

"Sure, you could do anything you wanted."

"But I can relax now. I have days off, I have time to enjoy my life, to take walks, to see plays, to have long lunches. Why should I focus all my time on being productive so that someday I can enjoy my life? I'm enjoying it now."

I overlooked that Jacob already had the life I was telling him he could enjoy someday, if only he worked more. And I realized that while I was supposed to be relaxing and having coffee, I had fallen into the trap of thinking about productivity, emphasizing work over play.

❖ ❖ ❖

Work and play do not have to be completely separate activities. It is good to find the fun in your work. Finding enjoyment in daily tasks helps us get through the day and through our lives. Unfortunately, it's too easy to become purely goal-driven and then unhappy when we don't reach every one of our goals.

While looking for the fun in our work, we must also strive to get the work out of our fun. For instance, one man asked, "But how about this? Instead of working all day Saturday and not having any time for my wife, I take my laptop computer out in the yard and work for four or five hours. She and I get to be together. That's how I work play into my schedule."

This man's wife would probably agree that he isn't doing much playing. She probably feels fairly neglected. Yes, she gets to be with his body, but is she with his mind, his heart? Are his heart and mind playing in the backyard, or are they coming up with the agenda for Monday's meeting? The man isn't playing, he's simply working in a different environment.

The ubiquitous cell phone has turned a great deal of fun time into work time. We have work conversations while eating in restaurants. We don't just drive, we drive and talk. People don't just shop anymore, they march up and down the mall with a phone glued to their ear. Some have been known to take calls during movies. One woman was overheard making calls on her cell phone while she was in labor.

Some of us even manage to turn hobbies and fun activities into work. One evening, a woman in remission from cancer was telling her husband about her overwhelming duties managing the local high school's annual show. Tired and drained, she thought back to what she had promised herself when she was ill.

"I thought becoming involved with the talent show would be fun," she said, "but now I'm being superproductive, I'm running everything. All I think and talk about are my duties. When I was afraid my time was limited, I promised myself that I would have more fun if I pulled through. Well, this isn't fun, it's work. If the cancer comes back, I won't be able to say that I've really enjoyed the time I have been given."

We've forgotten what hobbies are for. You may enjoy making furniture for its own sake, then suddenly think, "I could turn this into a business." It's great that you have a job doing something you love, but the very definition of a hobby is that you do it for fun without caring about the outcome. When you build furniture to sell, it's no longer a hobby—it's work. Without realizing it, you've contorted an activity you love into something you barely recognize and no longer do just for the fun of it.

We forget to play when we take life too seriously. We must remember a time when we played purely, before we learned to play productively. A time when our hearts were open and we could play without a sense of guilt afterward. But the idea of living to have fun is looked upon with suspicion. Early on we're told, "Life is serious, wipe that smile off your face. Do something, become something!" We look down on someone who is "just a surfer" and wonder why he doesn't make something of his life.

Wow! What a horrible life that must be: making your needs so minimal that you can do what you enjoy doing all day long. We think a surfer is inferior when he says he lives in a world where the fun never stops. The real question is, why do so many of us live in a world where the fun never starts?

Most everyone has heard that "play is the devil's work-shop" and knows it's "business before pleasure." As we climb up the ladder of success, we forget how to treat ourselves to fun. We see life as difficult, we want constantly to "improve" and "fix" things, we don't know how to take time off for just fun. We lose our familiarity with fun, and then, when we have some, we feel guilty. We discount fun as a waste of time. Perhaps that explains why so many successful people sneak out somewhere to play, and why the natural desire to have fun comes out in unhealthy ways in some people—people we see on the evening news. Many of us are like those workers in the office with the balloons; we have suppressed the need to play for so long it seeps out in our having affairs, using drugs, eating or shopping compulsively. We feel we don't deserve to have fun or be happy, so we sabotage our lives. We must learn to let ourselves be "bad," to have some fun.

Many of us were raised in families in which we were regularly asked, "What did you do today?" In response, we had to list all our accomplishments to prove we were productive and did not waste our time. Even now, as adults, we feel much more comfortable listing the tasks we've accomplished than we do saying we did something purely for pleasure. Ronnie Kaye, a cancer survivor, shares with groups how she had to learn to "admit" to others that she had just spent the afternoon listening to Beethoven. She says, "I had to learn to say with pride that I listened to Beethoven's Sixth Symphony all afternoon because it brings me great joy. I've cultivated friends who understand the importance of joy and say 'Good for you' when I tell them I've listened to music. There was a time when I would have been embarrassed about not doing a hundred other things. Now I realize how important music is to me."

We can play again no matter how old we may be, no matter what our situation. We can always find our sense of play again because it is always inside us.

Kids know how to play. In school, kids have recess because everyone agrees that schoolwork has to be balanced with fun. The same is true for adults. Why shouldn't we make play dates with each other?

Begin by learning to value play and playtime, and then give it to yourself. If you're a type A personality, you may have to schedule playtime and sometimes even "force" yourself to play. There's always more work to be done, but that's not a reason not to play. If you don't give yourself playtime, you ultimately won't have anything to give to anyone else. If you're not giving quality fun time to yourself, you'll begin to resent the time you give to the boss. You may even resent the time you give your family. Play now or pay later.

Remember that play is more than a lighthearted moment here and there, it's actual time devoted to play. You have to get away from work, get away from life's seriousness. There are a million ways to introduce play back into your life. Instead of checking the stock market first thing in the morning, read the comics. See a silly movie, buy a fun outfit. Wear a colorful tie. If your life or work is conservative, wear fun underwear. Practice saying yes to invitations, be more spontaneous. Do something silly.

Anything can be play, but beware: any form of play can also be turned into productivity. If you take walks because you truly enjoy them, they are play. If you're walking daily because it's part of the exercise routine you feel you must do, you're not playing.

Sports and games are wonderful sources of play. They bring out the kid in us, they can help us build identities, release stress, and connect with one another, whether we're running around a soccer field or concentrating on a bridge hand.

Many people hold game parties, inviting friends over to play Monopoly, Trivial Pursuit, or Risk. The guests are surprised at how much fun they have and how many wonderful memories these games recall. Competition is often a vital element of sports and games; it can be a wonderful motivator. It's only when we take it too seriously that we lose the joy of playing. Ever played a board game with someone who took it too seriously? It's no fun. Neither is life when we take it too seriously.

♣DK

I learned a lesson from my then four-year-old goddaughter, Emma. One day, little Emma was playing a game called Candyland with her friend Jenny. When Jenny was one step away from winning, Emma jumped up excitedly and said, "Oh Jenny, I hope you win!"

❖ ❖ ❖

Emma didn't understand the concept of beating the other person. For her, the fun was in the experience of playing the game. She didn't realize yet that if her friend won, she would lose. She was just happy to be playing. We could all learn a lot from her innocence.

Celebrations are an obvious chance to have fun. Don't save joy for special occasions; celebrate at every opportunity. We give enough time to the bad events; let's give equal, or even more, time to the good ones. Celebrate a friend coming over.

Celebrate a good meal. Celebrate Friday. Celebrate life. Dress up for no reason, get out the good china for yourself and family. We wouldn't hesitate to prepare an elaborate meal for strangers but often give ourselves only a can of tuna, a can opener, and some bread. Funerals are a particularly interesting example of this. Everyone is all dressed up, gathered at the bereaved's home. Everyone eats off the good china and sits in the living room that is otherwise never used. But did the deceased get to enjoy this stuff while he was alive?

Finally, give some time to yourself. Most of us agree that we need to spend quality time with loved ones. You also need quality time alone—time that is just for you. It's not the time when everyone else has left, or you happen to find yourself alone; it's time you've designated for yourself, time you give to you and your happiness. During your time you don't have to compromise on what movie you're seeing, what to eat, or what to do. This is the time you can be by yourself and for yourself, do what you want, when you want, and in just the way you want.

❖ EKR

Joe, an accomplished businessman, told me of his bout with lymphoma. "I had a large growth on my neck. It grew quickly. I saw a cancer specialist and immediately had the growth removed. Then the chemotherapy began. I went from being a productive worker to being a productive patient—monitoring lab tests, getting medications, keeping up with doctor visits. I never knew having a disease could be so much work.

"As I sat through one of my last chemo treatments, I thought about returning to work. My work had been so serious, and now, with the cancer, my life had become so serious. It was all about surviving, and thank God I had. Then I wondered, 'For what? What have I been saved for? More business? More productivity?'

"I began to realize what a gray, empty life I had. Everyone I knew had built their lives on being successful. I was just another brick in the wall. I decided I wasn't going back to that life.

"I decided to rebuild my life, to do things with friends, to find fun again. To go to the park and concerts, to watch people walking by, to occasionally chat with strangers instead of shutting everyone out. I had missed so much of life; it was time to enjoy it again."

When we were children, every experience was rich with possibilities for magic. If we could recapture just a touch of that old feeling and play a little more, we could regain some of our lost innocence. Even as our bodies grow older, we can stay young at heart. We can't help growing old on the outside, but if we keep playing, we'll stay young inside.

CHAPTER ELEVEN

THE LESSON
OF PATIENCE

J essica had one of those magical fathers—fun, adventur-
ous, and a little mischievous. But he was also unpredict-
able, often disappearing for weeks, even months, at a time
after he and Jessica's mother divorced.

Fourteen years old when her parents split permanently,
Jessica remained close to her father. Her mother was good
about explaining the father's absences. "That's just the way
he is," she would say. "It's not about you."

Jessica always knew her father was going to disappear
when he brought her a gift even though it wasn't her birthday or Christmas. Just as she would start to open it, her
father would stop her. "Patience, Jessica," he would say,
"this is a gift for later." After many days or weeks, when she
was really missing him, her mother would tell her to open
the gift.

As Jessica became a woman, her love for her father grew.
Even after she had finished school, become a marriage and
family counselor, and had a husband and two children of
her own, she and her seventy-something father were still as
close as ever. Whenever he was planning to disappear, he

would call to say that he was off on a trip and would see her when he got back.

One day he left and did not return. A few months passed and Jessica became very concerned; she felt something was different this time. When his friends told her that they had not heard from him in a long time either, she filed a missing persons report.

Four years later the call came. Her father had been found living in a nursing home in Las Vegas. Not until he had been admitted to a hospital for treatment of an acute infection had his name been noticed on a missing persons list. Oddly enough, the nursing home told Jessica that her father had repeatedly stated he had no family. Jessica was puzzled. But when she arrived in Las Vegas, she found out what was going on. Her father did not recognize her. He had Alzheimer's disease.

Jessica was glad to have found her father but heartbroken to learn of his condition. After he recovered from the infection, she arranged for him to be transferred to a care facility close to her home. She secretly hoped he would improve and remember her. "I thought that this was just like him, always trying my patience. I felt like I had found him, but in a strange way, I hadn't.

"I always thought that if I was just patient, sooner or later his memory would return. Day after day, week after week, I visited him. I was so angry; here he was and yet I didn't know this person and he didn't know me. The only thing that reminded me of my father was the patience it took to care for him. I tried to remember that the father I knew was in there, somewhere. As a counselor, I was always fixing other people's problems. My own problem, I couldn't fix. The only thing I could do was be patient."

Her father's physical condition slowly deteriorated. He came down with pneumonia and eventually died.

Over a year later, while preparing for a garage sale, Jessica came across her old answering machine. Her voice cracked as she said, "I thought I'd test it before putting it up for sale, so I plugged it in and pushed play. I couldn't believe what I heard. It was my father's last message. I had heard it when he left, but not since then. He said, 'Jessica, honey, just wanted to let you know I am leaving, I hope you always remember while I am gone, I think of you every day, even if we don't get to talk to each other. I know you worry about me, but I want you to know I am fine where I am. I love you dearly and look forward to seeing you again.' "

She wiped tears from her eyes. "That was my father— always teaching me patience. It was just like him to leave me one more gift, to be opened later."

Many situations and diseases, such as Alzheimer's, teach us big lessons in patience and understanding. Sometimes they are more for family and friends than for the ill.

❖ EKR

Patience is one of our hardest lessons, perhaps the most frustrating one to learn. I've never been a patient person. I've always been extremely busy, always on the move, traveling thousands of miles every year, seeing patients, giving lectures, writing books, raising my children.

Because of my illness, I can only get around in a wheelchair with someone's help and have been challenged with learning the lesson of patience. I hate that it's a lesson, yet I know that when we are sick, we must learn patience.

When I feel well enough, I go out with a friend. But I

want to move around, to get around faster than I can in a wheelchair. Sometimes, when we're in a store and someone's trying to get by, I feel that I'm in the way. And once, when I was out with a friend shopping for winter clothes, she left me there while she went looking in another aisle. I just had to be patient until she came back.

Now I often have to do one of the things I hate most—wait. When you're sick or dependent, everywhere you turn there is a lesson in patience. So I suppose it will be everywhere until I learn it. I'm truly having to learn this lesson from the inside out.

One lesson of patience is that you don't always get what you want. You may want something right now but may not get it for a while, if ever. You will, however, always get what you need, even if it does not fit into your mental picture.

In this modern world, people are not used to living with discomfort. We expect results and gratification, right now! We want answers faster than they can be delivered. There's twenty-four-hour repair and round-the-clock shopping. If we're hungry, there's always food available, from microwave dinners to all-night grocery stores and restaurants. There are twenty-four-hour office-supply and hardware stores, and who knows how much the Internet will supercharge our impatience? After all, we don't even have to go to a store to order a book, we don't have to drive up and down the streets with a real estate agent to see the houses for sale: it's all instantly available.

People no longer know how to wait, or even what waiting means. It's nice to have what you want when you want it, but the ability to delay gratification is important. Studies have shown that when children were given the choice of having one cookie now or two in an hour, the children who were able to wait did much better later in life. Patience is clearly an important asset, yet so many people stand in front of their microwaves thinking "Hurry up!" or are upset it if takes more than an hour to get their film developed.

The problem goes beyond the discomfort of having to wait. So many of us don't know how to live with things as they are, how to live in a situation just as it is. We feel we have to change it, make it better, we don't think things will be okay if they're left alone. We think there's a difference between something not happening soon enough and its not playing out the way we think it should. Yet these two thoughts come from the same place in the mind, from the judgment that the situation is wrong the way it is. What does being impatient ever get us?

The key to patience is knowing that everything is going to be fine, developing the faith that there is a plan. It is easy to forget this, and therefore many people try to control situations that would work out as they were meant to in their own perfect time. Even at the end of life, some accept that death is coming while others become impatient and want to know when. They are reassured to hear that they will not die before they are ready.

This is true about death and it is true about life. You will not be given any life experience before you are ready, when you find the trust and develop the understanding that things are moving the way they're supposed to and in their own time. Then you can relax.

Philosophically, patience is like a muscle that must regularly be used, it must be exercised and trusted. If we don't practice using the muscle in little, everyday situations—such as letting the tea take a minute or two to heat in the microwave—we won't have a strong muscle to support us through life's bigger challenges. That's why it's so important to develop a deep faith that healing is always at work. Since the mind will always seek to change things, we need to reassure ourselves that things are happening exactly as they're supposed to.

The mind wants to believe that changing our circumstances will bring us peace. The mind thinks we've got to do something. But the reality is that we can relax in the circumstances as they are now, knowing that deep patience will bring deep peace and healing.

Cancer survivor and talk show host Selma Shimmel, author of *Cancer Talk,* tells of her father, who says, "We think the alarm clock wakes us up every morning, but it is God who decides to wake us up." We think that we must determine the proper wake-up time, set the alarm, check it twice. We forget there is a bigger picture. God decides if we will have another day of life to wake up to. That is the bigger picture we miss, the muscle we don't use. Sure, set the alarm, but remember there is so much more at work than you realize.

❖EKR

Renee was waiting for the results of a biopsy. At first, she was completely focused on the two days she had to wait to find out if she had cancer. "Why is it taking so long?" she demanded over and over. "Can't they do a rush? What if it takes ten days? What if my doctor doesn't call back after a few days?"

I answered, "Whether we like it or not, it takes two days. Rather than spending two days fighting what is, ask yourself if there may be some important work to do in those two days. You can learn a lot about life in two days like these."

That's not to say, however, that you must wait forever. If the results are not back on time, you can call and say, "It's day three, what's happening with my results?" Being patient does not mean that we have to be victims. Being patient does not mean being powerless, it doesn't mean that we have to tolerate abuse or suffer through terrible circumstances. We can be patient and stand in our power at the same time.

The call came on time and everything was fine. "I learned about my power," Renee said later. "I learned to be with the process, to be with my feelings, to hear what the messages were. I learned to trust the universe and myself. I saw how, in the past, I didn't trust myself to find my power and use it if necessary. And I learned what to fix and what to accept. It was a great lesson."

❖ ❖ ❖

Renee was able to let the two days be and find a lot of strength in the waiting. She learned a lot about herself and her life when she was willing to be with the process and let it be. She also had to trust that if the results were not announced to her in two days, she had the power to call or go to her doctor.

It's important that we all find our power; if you're being victimized you should stand up and say, "This is not okay." But when life is dictating the story line, we need to find a way to relax in the situation as it is.

Life is a series of experiences everyone goes through. There is a reason for every experience, even if we don't see it; there is a point to it all. Everything that has happened has occurred so that we can get the lessons we need. But it is difficult for us to learn those lessons when we're impatiently screaming, "I don't like this! I want it to change!"

Sometimes we just have the experience, rather than deny, complain about, or try to change it.

Every experience will move us toward greater good and healing. The wonderful news is we don't have to do anything to get this right. We simply live life as it is happening.

A truck driver named Gary learned a lesson about patience. Always on the go, he had spent many years drinking to assuage his unhappiness. Now forty years old, he was threatened with the loss of his sight. "I had window blinds in my home. All of a sudden they began to look wavy, then I noticed spots in my vision. At first, I thought I was just tired."

The doctors implanted a new drug directly into his eye. It stopped the sight-robbing virus, but by that time this young man had already lost 65 percent of his vision. A secondary eye infection almost cost him his left eye completely. Two operations saved it, but his vision was severely damaged, and there was no hope of restoring it to normal.

Gary said, "I was told from the beginning there was nothing else to do about the eyesight. I knew I might spend a lifetime dealing with this.

"I needed a place to stay when I was in New York for treatment. By chance, the only place I could afford was a convent. It was full but they found one more room for me. While I was there, I prayed a lot for patience. I began to understand that I couldn't change what was happening. I had done everything, I had tried everything. There was nothing else I could do for my sight.

"In life we often lose things; this was my thing to lose. I have seen so many people dwell in the sad parts of their life. I would mourn, but I didn't want to spend the rest of my life mourning. Perhaps it was just the challenge I needed. Losing my vision slowed me down and made me refocus.

"I continued in a way I wouldn't have before. Before I would have sat around doing nothing, being unhappy, drinking. But now I had to learn all kinds of new things to stay alive, including how to move through problems. No one was taking care of me, I had to do it myself. I had to find my own dreams and goals. It made me experience life more, enjoy it much more. I loved to play pool but thought I'd have to stop. But with some practice, I became good at it again. I have noticed that people in Los Angeles, where I live, are very impatient. They don't have time, they want to rush, rush, rush. I used to be one of them but now I see that time is there to enjoy. And there is so much of it to enjoy.

"In some ways, I see more now than I did when I had all my sight. I look harder. I have to look harder now. I look for the humor and the good stuff in everything. A lot of people just can't find the good things or the humor in life. I don't think I see things that other people can't see, they just don't have the patience to look or notice."

The first step in becoming more patient is giving up the need to fix or change things—it is having the awareness that some things are the way they are for a reason, even if we don't think so or can't see it.

If something is not changeable, try to see it as not broken. Try to find a little faith in the process and the unfolding of things. Despite our belief that things need our assistance, most of the amazing things that happen in the world occur without our help, interference, or assistance. We don't have to tell the cells in our bodies to divide, we don't have to tell a cut to heal. There is a power in the world. Trust that all things are moving toward the good, even when we don't recognize it or see it. That is faith. Having patience is having faith.

In faith, you remember that no experience is wasted. Most people at the end of life would not even trade in their bad experiences, for they learned from everything that happened to them. Everything you go through, every windstorm in life, happens so that the perfect you can be born. If things are moving too fast or slow for you, remember that your timing hasn't always been the greatest, and that there is a plan. You can afford to relax and let life unfold.

To afford means it is within our ability to give. This is a reminder that it is within our ability to relax and give in to the situation, knowing that we have the time, means, and courage to wait. And to remember that there may be nothing to wait for, that this may be the situation exactly as it's supposed to be. It is no accident that the noun *patient,* meaning person undergoing medical treatment, and the adjective *patient,* meaning to tolerate affliction with calmness, are connected. They come from the Latin word *pati,* which means to endure.

We may think the story is about our health, work, or love life, and want to change it. Remember that it is not about those things, it is about you. It's about the love, compassion, humor, and patience you bring to your life and its situations.

And remember that God and the universe are not ultimately just working on the situation: they're working on you. If you're wondering why the universe isn't solely focused on getting you the great job offer, it's because the universe isn't always concerned with which job you have. The picture is much bigger than your job. Neither is the universe always concerned whether or not you're married—it's more concerned with your experience of love than who is or is not in your life. And rather than focusing solely on your health, the universe is more concerned with your experience of life, whatever the conditions may be. The universe is concerned with who you are, and it will bring into your life, in whatever the situations, in whatever time, what you need to become the person you're supposed to be. They key lies in trusting—and having patience.

CHAPTER TWELVE

THE LESSON
OF SURRENDER

❖EKR

I remember well one young boy I worked with as he was dying. Toward the end of his life he drew a picture of himself as a tiny figure, about to be struck by a large cannonball. This showed that he saw his disease as a destructive force. He knew he was going to die, but he had clearly not reached a place of peace.

After we worked together for a while, he accepted and surrendered to what was happening in his body. I knew our work was done when he drew a picture of himself flying on the wings of a bird to heaven. Now he felt a loving force would carry him off; he wouldn't resist it. This surrender made the rest of his life, however brief, more enjoyable and meaningful.

❖ ❖ ❖

At any time we can all find a wonderful peace in surrender. Unfortunately, too many of us are afraid of it because it's giving up and giving in, it's a sign of weakness. But there is no weakness or pain in surrender. Instead, there is comfort and strength in surrendering to the knowledge that all is well, all is being taken care of.

It can take a lot of faith to imagine that all is well in the midst of disease or loss. Even in the small trials of life, it is hard to surrender. We want to handle situations, we want to make things happen. We equate activity with strength, passivity with weakness. The idea that letting go may be positive can be difficult until we realize that much of life is supposed to be lived with ease. We are not supposed to be in situations where we are banging our heads against the wall. If we are constantly struggling, perhaps the universe is trying to tell us something. We can let ourselves relax. We needn't constantly seize hold of the job, relationship, or situation. We can simply relax, knowing that life will unfold as it is supposed to.

Think of life as a roller coaster. We ride the coaster, we don't drive it. Can you imagine how frustrating it would be to try to make the roller coaster go the way you want it to? Not only would you not be able to steer it, you would miss the experience of just riding it, with all of its highs and lows.

The signal to surrender comes when we are exhausted from trying to control a situation or win a battle. We surrender so we can let go of that death grip. To stop the worrying. To stop the constant fighting, which is so destructive. It takes us out of the moment, prevents joyful relationships, destroys creativity, and disrupts our happiness and contentment. The struggle creates fear, which gives us the false belief that we must control every aspect of our lives, all the time. Now is the time to surrender, to ride the horse in the direction it is going, to swim with the current, not against it.

Dale was a middle-aged man battling heart disease. He

shared, "I have lived this long, in good health, because I have been able to surrender.

"I learned years ago that we just make things worse if we don't surrender. At first I thought it was a contradiction. How could I surrender, relax, and take life easy when I knew I had severe heart disease and could die any minute? How could I relax into a bad situation? And how would that help? Then I felt my father with me. He had been dead for many years, but I still feel him in my heart and soul from time to time.

"My father was a good man who died from cancer. He had almost died years before from alcoholism. He lost jobs because of his drinking, he caused enormous problems for my mother. He needed help to save his life, but when someone is dying of alcoholism, we often just see the drinking and forget they are dying. Besides, nothing could change unless he was willing to admit that he had a problem and surrendered his struggle to a higher power. He had to accept the knowledge that he was an alcoholic. He couldn't have stopped drinking any other way.

"He finally joined Alcoholics Anonymous and changed his life. He went on to get a degree in psychology from UCLA, then counseled people in prisons. He was able to do so much good because he knew what it was like to need help—especially with surrender and acceptance.

"When he died, hundreds of people came to his funeral. They loved him—all those people he had helped by not giving up, but giving in. I was so proud of him. I saw that the lesson he had learned applied to me, too. I had to relax into my diagnosis of heart disease. I had to surrender into what is. I had to come out of denial and quit fighting the unfightable. I had no choice of having or not having heart disease, that was a fait accompli. By surrendering, I could find peace and quality in life again."

Many of us labor under the illusion that control is always good, that it would be dangerous to just let the universe take care of things. But is our control really necessary to the workings of the world? We don't have to wake up early every morning to remind the universe to make the sun rise; when we turn our backs on the ocean, the universe doesn't mess up and make the tide go the wrong way. We don't have to remind our children to grow every year, hold seminars for flowers to explain how to bloom, or make sure the planets maintain their distance from each other. The universe runs this amazingly complex planet, with all its flowers, trees, animals, winds, sunshine, and everything else, quite well, yet this is the power we are afraid to surrender into. It may sometimes be hard to find the good or the lesson in a difficult situation; we may wonder why it's happening. But there is often no other way for the universe to heal us except to present us with the tough situations. Try to see it as what *is,* rather than what is *bad*. None of us really knows why events happen in our lives. The problem is that we think we should know; but living requires humility, for life is a mystery. All will be revealed in its own time.

How do we surrender? How do we stop fighting? It is like ending a game of tug-of-war—we simply let go. We let go of our way. We learn to trust in God, in the universe, as we begin, for the first time in our lives, to relax.

In letting go, we release our mental pictures of how things should turn out and accept what the universe brings us. We accept that we don't really know how things should be. The dying learn this as they look back on their life. They see that "bad" situations often led them to better places, and that what they thought was good wasn't necessarily best for them. For example, wonderful experimental therapies can work and become wondrous ways of healing. They can also fail, causing more harm than good. Many patients have fought to get on experimental therapies, certain that they would save their life. Sometimes they were right, sometimes they weren't. The truth is that we don't always know what is in our best interest. That's why we have to let go of wanting to know where life is going to take us, we have to stop insisting that we always know what is right and must stop trying to control the uncontrollable. Those times we thought we absolutely knew what was best, we were wrestling with illusions. We have never known, and never will.

To surrender we simply rise every day and say "thy will," not "my will." We say, "I don't know what's supposed to happen today. Yes, I have a plan for the day, I will go to work, I will mow the lawn, et cetera. But I surrender to the knowledge that my plans are just a working blueprint. There will be changes, paths I didn't expect. Wonderful surprises, maybe scary surprises. There will be situations that will lead me on new journeys. I trust that all this will lead me in a direction that will bring my being, my soul, to its greatest unfolding."

❖ D K

James, a spry man of seventy-four with Parkinson's disease, had been very active throughout life. He gave and gave and gave, but never learned how to receive. When he became sick enough that others had to take care of him, he could no longer see any reason for living. His family explained to him that it was a joy for them to be able to provide loving care. As much as they wished this tragic situation wasn't happening, they felt it was an honor to give back to him. But he, only seeing himself as a victim, seriously considered suicide as a way out.

When we talked about his feelings, I said, "No one can stop you from killing yourself, if that's what you are going to do. But what seems to be bothering you most is the feeling that you've lost the ability to choose. Is there any way you can see that while you can kill yourself, you can also choose not to? You can choose to stay in this situation, and this can be a positive kind of surrender. Not positive in the sense that it's a great thing, but positive in that you are choosing surrender for a greater purpose. You are making a choice, you are not a victim."

Knowing that James was a veteran, I asked what he had done in the war. "I was a pilot," he said proudly.

Armed with this knowledge, I continued, "James, I understand you want to have control and don't want to surrender into this. But haven't there been flying situations where you've had to yield in a positive way?"

He thought for a moment, then replied, "Yes. I had to submit to the control of the tower. I knew that the air traffic controllers had a much bigger picture of what's going on, so I gladly turned things over to them."

"Then can you believe that in this situation there may be a bigger picture in your life, and in your loved one's lives? Maybe these lessons just aren't for you, maybe they're for everyone. Just like the traffic controller was concerned with every plane in the sky, not just yours?"

That seemed to make all the difference for him. He understood that surrender was a choice, and that it did not mean giving up.

❖ ❖ ❖

There's an important difference between surrender and just plain quitting. To give up is to throw our hands up in the air and say, "There's no hope, I'm dead!" when diagnosed with a terminal illness. To surrender is to choose the treatments that feel right and, if they don't work, to accept that our time here is limited. When we give up, we deny the life we have. When we surrender, we accept it just as it is. To be a victim of disease is to give up. But to see that we always have choices, in every situation, is surrender. To turn away from the situation is to give up. To turn into it is surrender.

✤EKR

God was shrewd: my head was not affected by my strokes. Talk about a way to teach lessons. I can't use my left leg and arm, but I can talk and I can think.

Many times, people lose function on the whole left side, including the ability to speak well. But not me; from the neck up I'm completely intact and fine. Yet the left side of my body is paralyzed, which is why I call my stroke paradoxical. There's no mental impact, but the left side of my body, the feminine side, is underdeveloped. The feminine side is the side that receives. Pink is considered a feminine color, and it's no accident that I hate it! But now I'm trying to learn to appreciate it.

I must work on receiving, on learning to say thank you. I must learn patience and surrender. Throughout my life, I have given and given, but never learned to receive. This is my lesson now, learning to receive love, receive care, to be nurtured rather than nurturing. I realized I had a big stone wall around my heart. It was designed to protect me from hurt, but it also kept the love out.

❖ ❖ ❖

Many people have difficulty submitting positively even in life's little situations. We probably all know people who, even at a lecture, feel they must stand up and challenge the speaker.

"I *have* to set things straight," they might say. "The speaker was wrong."

People like this don't get the idea of just being a listener and receiver. They do not realize they don't have to disagree, they don't have to set everyone straight. Instead, they could give the speaker a chance to present the material and, perhaps, change their mind a little. After they experienced the material as a whole, if they said, "I disagree with it" or "I won't listen to this speaker again," that would be fine. But if you start disagreeing right away, you don't allow yourself to surrender into receiving and learning.

Some believe that even to listen to what someone else has to say means losing a fight. The truth is, to have listened, and listened carefully, would have been a brief, positive surrender to someone else's point of view, which could be incorporated into their own, investigated further, or set aside.

A maître d' at a well-known restaurant tells how customers come in and say, "I want to try your famous Caesar salad, but with plain oil and vinegar" or "I want your chicken special, only grilled, not broiled, and without the sauce."

This maître d' said, "What we bring to the meal is our unique way of cooking and presenting it. If you don't receive it as we present it, you're missing the very thing our chef does so well. I understand when someone has had it once and maybe then would like it with less sauce or has real dietary restrictions, but many times they just don't give us a chance to present it our way."

We have all become so very controlling. We have forgotten what it's like to be students and to sit at the feet of others. We don't know how to receive other ideas and experiences, even if only for a brief while, even the little things in life.

Refusing to accept situations we cannot change exhausts us, strips us of our power and peace of mind. We take back our power and regain peace of mind when we let things be as they are. We are, in effect, saying, "I am going to be happy right now. I'm not going to put it off."

Refusing to surrender, on the other hand, is the same as saying, "I can't possibly be happy until the conditions change. No way, no how." Perhaps new conditions would be more pleasurable. But the conditions may never change, which makes us victims of their not changing. To say, "I will only be peaceful if such and such happens" is pretty limiting. Is the situation you imagine really the only "good" one? Aren't there many other circumstances and situations that would bring peace? Some of which you haven't even thought of?

I'm not talking about accepting everything that happens. If you don't like the television show you're watching, you don't have to surrender to it—change the channel. If you don't like your job, look for a new one. Fix your car if you think it rattles too much. If you're unhappy with a situation that should be corrected, find your power and make the correction.

I'm talking about situations we have decided are insurmountable obstacles to happiness. We insist that we absolutely cannot be happy unless these situations change—but they can't be. If you've had a bad childhood, you can't go back and make it a happy one. If someone you love does not return your love, you can't force love. If you have cancer right now, you are not cancer-free at this moment.

In these situations we can be as unhappy as unhappy can

be, but we will never change the facts. Surrendering into life as it is can be the quickest and most powerful way to get the lesson out of the situation. You can't change your bad childhood, but you can have a good life. You can't make someone love you, but you can stop wasting your time and energy on him or her. You can't wave a magic wand and make your cancer disappear, but that doesn't mean life is over.

✦ D K

A diabetic man named Bryan was hospitalized for an infection in his right leg. The fifty-year-old corporate manager was wild with fear and filled with anger because the doctors told him that his leg might have to be amputated.

Bryan first needed permission to fully feel everything, then to let all those feelings out. When he had done that, I asked, "Can you surrender into the situation as it is?"

At first, Bryan saw nothing beneficial in this idea; he was angry that I had even brought it up. I continued, however, saying, "The horrible possibility that you may lose your leg is constantly on your mind, it's dominating your thoughts, it's filling you with fear and anger. Why not think about it for a while, be with it, then let it be? If you're going to lose your leg, you're going to lose your leg. Thinking about it, pretending that you are not thinking about it, or refusing even to talk about it isn't going to make it happen or not happen."

"So if I make peace with losing my leg, if I completely surrender, will it be saved?"

I reminded him that deep spiritual work is deep spiritual work. We can't bargain with it, we can't say, "If I'm spiritual enough, will I get the prize?" If Bryan surrendered to the idea of losing his leg, he might still lose it. But this possible leg amputation was a demon holding him hostage, along with his happiness and his ability to grow from the situation. The idea of losing his leg was so terrifying, he couldn't think about it right away.

But when he was finally able to look at the situation with his feelings and wonder, "I might lose my leg. What would it be like if I did?" Bryan realized that he would get through. He would get an artificial leg and life would continue. Once he was through to the other side of surrender, he found some peace. He relaxed into the situation, helping his body heal and move in whatever direction he was supposed to. Luckily, his leg responded well to treatment and was saved. Looking back, though, Bryan says that the most amazing part of the horrible situation was that when he finally surrendered to the worst possible scenario, he found peace.

❖ ❖ ❖

We insist that we can't possibly be happy until tomorrow, when things change. But if happiness is possible tomorrow, it is also possible today. If love is possible tomorrow, it is possible today. We can find healing even if nothing changes. To surrender to life "as is" can miraculously transform situations. It is in this surrender that we are able to receive. The universe gives us the tools to fulfill our destinies when we let things be.

When is the right time to surrender? In what situations? Every day, every moment, and every situation is an opportunity for surrender. We surrender to a force bigger than we are when we are born and again when we die. Between life and death we get lost because we forget to surrender.

If something should be changed and you have the power to change it, go ahead. But learn to recognize the situations that cannot be changed. They are the times when we feel as if we are bailing against the tide, when we struggle and are afraid. These are the times when we must accept and surrender, or our struggle consumes us.

If you don't feel at peace, it's time to surrender.

If life doesn't flow, it's time to surrender.

If you feel that you're responsible for everything, it's time to surrender.

If you want to change what cannot be changed, it's time to surrender.

And when you do opt for change, think carefully about exactly what needs to be different, and why. Steve, for instance, was unhappy being an accountant because he really wanted to be in the theater. He constantly struggled with himself because he was unwilling to give up the security and certainty of his professional career for the unstable life of the theater. When he finally accepted that he would remain an accountant, someone told him that a theater company was looking for a new chief financial officer. Steve got the job and is now one of the biggest and most successful chief financial officers specializing in Broadway shows.

Letting things be instead of constantly struggling to make them happen is a wonderful gift we give to ourselves. If we look back on life, we will see that some of our best moments and greatest opportunities did not come out of the struggle to set things right. They seem like lucky coincidences, as if they occurred because we were in the right places at the right times. That is how surrender works, and that is how life works: subtly.

So many people who want to change what they are come to the realization that a shoemaker makes shoes, remembering that we can bring incredible style, creativity, and worth to the way we make the shoes, instead of trying to do something else.

Sometimes the need to change is obvious, sometimes it's not. When we don't know if it's time to surrender, the serenity prayer can be helpful:

God,
Grant me the serenity to accept the things I cannot change, the
courage to change the things I can, and the wisdom to know the
difference.

Sometimes people learn the lesson of surrender in unexpected ways and places. "When I was twenty-seven, I worked in Japan," Jeff said. "It was an exciting place to be, right on the cutting edge of business. In the midst of this huge project, I began to lose my appetite; then I was feeling tired. I just thought it was because of all the work. I was finally hospitalized and treated for pneumonia. I thought that was bad until they told me this type of pneumonia was caused by HIV. The doctors stabilized me enough for a trip back to the United States.

"When I was sent home to America, I only brought a few things in my green backpack. All my other possessions were left behind. My old life was also left behind: I had studied Japanese business for years, I had always wanted to live in Japan. After I had recovered from pneumonia, I thought about how all my dreams had just been snatched away. It was like being told, 'Sorry, you can't have what you want anymore.' And it was true. I couldn't have that. It would just have been too difficult to be in a foreign country, away from the treatment and monitoring I needed. It is hard enough to navigate the health-care system in this country.

"At first I was angry and frustrated. But I saw I still had some sense of choice. I could try to live the old, now impractical dream, or I could surrender into this new life. It would have produced enormous stress to try to hold on to my old life. It was time to surrender. I had been given a new life.

"After I quit fighting the reality of what is, new ideas and dreams began to surface. The lawyers I worked with had always impressed me, and I realized that I could be a lawyer. Law school takes three years, but thanks to the medical care I had a future. In that surrender I saw parts of myself that I had never seen before: my courage, my adaptability. I now have a wonderful life. And I see how things are perfect. I love being back here in the States, everything feels so right. I have settled down here in a way I never expected to. So many new and wonderful possibilities popped up when I surrendered into this new future."

Jeff could have felt angry and victimized by his situation for the next twenty years. He chose not to, instead surrendering into what life had given him. Even he was surprised by his lack of bitterness when we spoke. "I would have predicted that I would be bitter," he said. "But learning that I have the capability to see things differently and let go of my preconceptions has been a wonderful gift. The clichés have all become true. Life is too short, we don't know when our last day is. To find the good in the bad is one of the most rewarding lessons I've learned."

CHAPTER THIRTEEN

THE LESSON
OF FORGIVENESS

During the late 1940s, India was engulfed in religious wars as the nation prepared for independence from Great Britain. A Hindu whose son was murdered by Muslims during the internal strife went to see Mahatma Gandhi and asked, "How can I possibly forgive the Muslims? How can I ever find peace again with so much hate in my heart for those who have killed my only son?"

Gandhi suggested that the man adopt an orphaned enemy child and raise him as his own.

We need to forgive so that we can live whole lives. Forgiveness is the way to heal our hurts and wounds, it's how we reconnect with others and ourselves. We have all been hurt—we didn't deserve the pain, but were wounded nonetheless. And, if truth be told, we have almost certainly hurt others. The problem isn't that hurt happens, it's that we can't or won't forget it. This is the hurt that keeps on hurting. We go through life accumulating these hurts; we have no training or guidance in how to let them go. This is where forgiveness comes in.

We have a choice to live in forgiveness or unforgiveness.

Forgiveness can ironically be a selfish act in that it matters more to the wounded than to those who did the wounding. The dying often find a peace they lacked in life because dying is letting go; so is forgiving. When we do not forgive, we hang on to old wounds, hurts, and upsets. We keep the unhappy parts of the past alive and feed our resentments. When we don't forgive, we become slaves to ourselves.

Forgiveness offers us much, including that sense of wholeness we are sure was permanently taken from us by the offender. It offers us a freedom to again be who we are. We all deserve the chance to give ourselves and our relationships a fresh start. That chance is the magic of forgiveness. Once we forgive others, or ourselves, we are restored to a place of grace. Just as a broken bone is stronger than before the break when it heals, our relationships and our lives can be stronger when forgiveness heals our wounds.

The dying can teach us much about genuine forgiveness. They do not think, "I have been so right, and in being so right, I can see how wrong you have been. In my bigness I will forgive you." They think, "You've made mistakes and so have I. Who hasn't? But I no longer want to define you by your mistakes or have me be defined by mine."

There are many blocks to forgiveness. Chief among these is the feeling that by forgiving we are condoning the behavior that hurts us.

But to forgive is not to say, "It's okay that you hurt me." It means we let the hurt go for our own sakes when we realize that holding on to grudges forces *us* to live in unhappiness. People who are reluctant to forgive need to remember that they are not punishing anyone except themselves.

Forgiveness does not mean letting people walk all over

us. It's about charity in the best sense of the word. When we forgive, we remember that someone was not at their best when they hurt us. We remember that they are more than their errors. They're human, they made mistakes, and they themselves have been wounded just as we were. Ultimately, forgiveness happens inside us. We forgive to heal ourselves. Someone else's behavior is someone else's behavior. We don't have to forgive the behavior, we only need to forgive the person.

The desire for revenge is another block to forgiveness. Getting even only gives us a temporary feeling of relief or satisfaction, if that. Then we feel guilty for lowering ourselves to the kind of behavior we thought was wrong in the first place. We want whoever hurt us to know how much we hurt, so we lash out—and then we only hurt more. There is nothing wrong with communicating our hurt; but again, it becomes self-punishment when we hang on to it.

It can be hard to forgive. Sometimes it's easier to ignore the situation. Many times we have the urge to forgive but we put it off, passively allowing a stream of misery to trickle through our lives. It may not be until our lives are challenged that we realize we don't want to live like this, and that we may not have forever to clear the water.

Unforgiveness keeps us stuck. We know this old terrain well and may have become so comfortable with it that forgiveness can feel like venturing into the unknown. It is often easier to blame someone than to repair a relationship. With our eyes focused on their mistakes, we don't have to look at ourselves and our issues. In forgiveness we take back our power to live and flourish beyond an offending incident. Living in the hurt keeps us perpetual victims; in forgiveness we transcend the hurt. We don't have to be permanently wounded by anyone or anything. There is great power in this awareness.

Telling you how to forgive in a few easy steps is like telling you how to save the world—it's that hard to do. Forgiving can feel gut-wrenching; that's why sometimes it feels like trying to save the world. By the way, that *is* how you save the world.

When, as children, we got hurt or hurt others, someone usually said, "I'm sorry." Now that we're adults, these apologies don't come so often. And sometimes, when they do come, we decide they're not enough. When children do wrong, we see their fear, their confusion, their lack of knowledge. We see them as human. But as adults we tend to see those who hurt as what they did to us. They become one-dimensional characters defined only by the pain they have caused. The first step in forgiving is to see them as human beings again. They make mistakes; at times they're weak, insensitive, confused, and in pain. They're faulty, fragile, lonely, needy, and emotionally imperfect. In other words, they're just like us. They are souls on a journey filled with ups and downs.

Once we can acknowledge they are human, we can begin to forgive them by becoming aware of our anger. We must get that blocked energy out by yelling into a pillow, telling a friend how angry we are, screaming, or doing whatever else it takes to let it out. Then, often, we will find the sadness, pain, hate, and hurt that was underneath the anger. When we do, we must let ourselves feel these feelings. Next comes the hardest part: letting those feelings go. Forgiveness is not about the people who hurt you; don't worry about them. Whatever they did was probably more about them, their world, and their problems than about us. In letting them off the hook *we* will find freedom. Everyone has issues to deal with, none of which is our business. Our business is our peace of mind, our happiness.

✤DK

Sometimes it seems impossible to forgive, for the act committed was too offensive. Here, Elisabeth Mann could us teach many lessons about tolerance, love, anger, and forgiveness.

Elisabeth has much to be angry about. When she was a teenager, she and her family were rounded up by the Nazis and sent to Auschwitz, a concentration camp where the average life expectancy was brief. Shortly after her arrival there, she asked a guard where the rest of her family was. He pointed to the smoke coming out of a massive chimney, saying, "That's where they are."

After the camp was liberated by Allied soldiers, Elisabeth found herself in Denmark, waiting for a train to Sweden. There were other survivors with her, but her family was gone. "I was given a cup of coffee that tasted so good, I've never had anything to match it," she declares. A nurse brought in two women and a man, saying they were also concentration camp survivors. "I suspected they were not, for they had bags with them. No one from a camp had luggage, we didn't even have an extra piece of cloth. These two women and the man started asking us questions about which camp we came from, how we got here. My fellow survivors shared their stories.

"The next morning the train arrived to take us to Sweden. I was put in a compartment with the two women who had asked the questions, plus three others. There wasn't a lot of room in the car, especially with the suitcases the two women had brought. The two of them sat on the floor, the three others took a bench, and I climbed overhead, in the place where you normally put the luggage. That night, when they thought everyone was sleeping, I heard a noise. Looking down, I saw that the two women had opened one of their suitcases, and inside were photos of people in SS uniforms. The women were tearing the pictures up and throwing them out the window. You have to understand that no one in a camp would have had, or even wanted to have, pictures of the guards.

"Some officials got on the train at one of the stops and asked us all questions. When he asked the two women and the man where they had been, which camp and so on, they recited the stories they had heard from my fellow inmates the night before. I could have said something, but I was so full of happiness that the war was over. I was convinced that every soul had learned from the war. I thought it was not my place to punish these people. If God wants to punish them, he will. We arrived in Sweden and I never saw them again.

"What I did was not to condone what these people had done. It was to trust God that forgiveness was in his hands, not mine. It wasn't my place to decide their fate. With all the people who had died, my little brother, my parents, how could I say, 'It's okay, it doesn't matter?'

"But it was important to me to never have the desire for revenge in my heart. I remember, in the camp, we would pass a bakery every morning as we were taken to clean the streets. We were always hungry, and that fresh-baked-bread aroma would hit us. We would say, 'When we are free, we will run to the bakery and eat up all the bread.' We never said we would run to the bakery and kill the baker."

Most things in our life are not as horrific as what happened during the Holocaust. Still, there are things we feel we should not forgive. When that happens, we can do what Elisabeth Mann did: give the situation to God. Although young, alone, and terribly vulnerable, she recognized it was God's place to judge, if that was His will. In other cases we truly want to forgive, but just can't bring ourselves to do it. Then it is good to ask for help: "God, I would like to forgive but I can't. Please help me."

❖ ❖ ❖

❖EKR

As much as we all may want to always be able to practice forgiveness, it is a daunting task. And as long as we're human, it may be impossible to completely forgive everybody for every single thing. I realize in my own life there are things I am having trouble forgiving, and if I don't forgive every little single thing by the time I die—that's okay, because I don't want to die a saint.

When I was still very sick and dependent, I had nurse's aides coming in to take care of me. I noticed they seemed to be throwing out an enormous amount of trash. Big plastic bags of trash every day. At the time, I was confined to bed and thought, "I just don't have that much trash!"

When I questioned them, they said they were just taking out the trash. It wasn't until later, when I was able to move around more, that I realized they were stealing from me every day. Not only were they taking things of monetary value, they were stealing the few mementos I still had after my last house burned down. Paintings, diplomas, and degrees were gone. I have a tough heart, so I didn't have a heart attack.

I should forgive, but I don't want to. Not yet. I'm not even working on it. Obviously, I'm not ready yet.

❖ ❖ ❖

Ironically, the person we most often need to forgive is ourselves. We have to forgive ourselves for what we have done, and for what we have not done. Anytime we think we have made a mistake, we must forgive ourselves; if we feel we haven't learned a lesson, we must forgive ourselves for not learning.

What we need to forgive ourselves for doesn't always make sense—it may not even have been a real mistake. Often, especially if we are young, we feel responsible for events around us—usually more than we should.

❖DK

Elisabeth Mann must still forgive herself daily for one of those tragic "what if" situations she was thrust into when she was so young.

When her family arrived at Auschwitz, they stood before armed guards who asked her how old her brother was. She told them that he was thirteen. She said proudly that according to the Jewish tradition, he was now a bar mitzvah, a man.

After realizing that the men were immediately sent to the gas chamber while the children were spared, she feared that her comment had marked her brother for death.

"I wish I had thought to say he was younger," she confesses. "Maybe if I hadn't said his real age, he would be alive; maybe if I hadn't said anything, he would have survived. I often feel like I sent him to his death."

To this day, Elisabeth misses her little brother and wonders "what if."

She must continue to find forgiveness in her heart from this misplaced sense of responsibility.

Most of us do not have to deal with issues as big as Elisabeth Mann's. But we do judge ourselves as inadequate or downright bad, often daily. A key to forgiving ourselves is realizing that we would have done things differently if we had seen a better way. No one decides, "Oh, this would be a good mistake to make" or "I'll do this because it will make me feel really bad about hurting someone." We thought we were doing the right thing, which is why we must forgive ourselves for not knowing everything. And even if we did hurt someone intentionally, it was probably because we were in pain. If we could have made better choices, we probably would have.

We are here in this life to make mistakes, to accidentally hurt one another, to get ourselves lost from time to time. If we were perfect, we wouldn't be here at all. And the only way to learn to forgive ourselves is to make a few mistakes. We did what we did because we are human. If we did something so terrible that we cannot forgive ourselves, we can always give it to God to handle. We can say, "God, I can't forgive myself yet. Can you forgive me and help me find forgiveness in myself?"

Remember that forgiveness is not a once-in-a-lifetime task, it is ongoing. It is our spiritual maintenance plan. Forgiveness helps keep us at peace and in touch with love. Our only task is to try to open our hearts again.

CHAPTER FOURTEEN

THE LESSON
OF HAPPINESS

❖ EKR

Terry, a forty-five-year-old man who had been diagnosed as terminally ill, was spending his last days in a hospice. When I met him, he told me he was doing quite well. Intrigued by his sunny disposition, I asked about his illness. He was not in denial; his response was clear and grounded in reality. So I asked, "How do you live with the knowledge of your death? We all know, intellectually, that we will die someday, but you live with the very real knowledge that you may die soon."

Terry replied, "I live very well with it. In fact, I am happier now than I ever imagined possible. Strange as it may seem, I was unhappy for most of my life. I just accepted that this was the best it could be. But now that my time is limited, I've really looked at life and decided that if I am alive, I want to be really alive; if I am dead, I want to be really dead. I've also thought about what I want to do before I leave. And in the midst of all this, I realize I am happier than I have been before."

❖ ❖ ❖

Something about the meaning of life changes when you realize deeply that it won't last forever. The opposite is also true: it is not unusual to hear from people in remission that they were actually happier when they thought their days were numbered. We bring a deeper commitment to our happiness when we fully understand, as Terry did, that our time left is limited and we really need to make it count.

Most of us think of happiness as a reaction to an event, but it is actually a state of mind that has very little to do with what is going on around us. Plenty of people have been sure they would be absolutely happy when they got or did something, only to become unhappy when the great event occurred. We have seen over and over that lasting happiness is not found in winning the lottery, having a beautiful body, or eliminating wrinkles. All these things are temporarily elating, but the thrill quickly wears off and we are soon as happy or unhappy as we were before.

The good news is we have been given all we need to make us happy; the bad news is we often don't know how to use what we've been given. Our minds, our hearts, and our souls have been fully coded for happiness; all the wiring is built-in. Everyone is capable of finding happiness. All he or she has to do is look for it in the right places.

While happiness is our natural state, we've been trained to feel more comfortable with unhappiness. In a strange way we are not used to happiness: at times it feels not only unnatural but undeserved. That's why we often find ourselves thinking the worst about someone or some situation. It's also why we must work to feel good about being happy and why we must commit ourselves to happiness.

Part of the work is accepting the belief that finding happiness is essentially our purpose of life. Many people recoil at such a thought, saying such an approach is self-centered and uncaring. Why do we resist the idea that the purpose of life is being happy?

We feel guilty being happy, and we wonder how we can strive to be happy when so many people are less fortunate than we are. Or, as someone bluntly put it, "Why should you be happy?"

The answer is that you are God's precious child. You were meant to enjoy all the wonders around you. And remember that you have more to give to others, to the suffering, when you are happy. When you have enough and are content, you will not act from a place of need or lack. You will feel that you have a little extra to give to those around you, that you can afford to share more of your time, yourself, your money, and your happiness.

In reality, happy people are the least self-absorbed and self-centered among us. They often volunteer their time and provide service to others, they are often kinder, more loving, forgiving, and caring than their unhappy counterparts. Being unhappy leads to selfish behavior, while happiness expands our capacity to give.

True happiness is not the result of an event, it does not depend on circumstance. You, not what's going on around you, determine your happiness.

A woman named Audrey realized this when she hosted a charity event for ALS, Lou Gehrig's disease. Not only was Audrey hosting the fund-raiser, she had the disease herself.

This was the second time she had volunteered to host the event. The first time, ten years earlier, she had just been diagnosed and knew she had many years of life ahead. By now her disease had progressed dramatically, so she knew this would be the last time she would be able to take on such a task.

"I wanted to do it once more," Audrey said. "I have learned so much in the last ten years. When I first did it, I felt as if I were being used. I didn't like being the ALS poster girl. This time I was older and wiser. The first time, I had been very naive. There were disagreements, there were egos, there was just a lot of crap. Now I would do better. I looked forward to it. But only a few weeks into the planning, the same things began to happen all over again. I didn't understand it. I was in tears. I couldn't do any better than I had done years earlier!

"I started to beat myself up. I was so sure I had grown and changed. Then it hit me: I had changed, but the circumstances had not. Why did I expect there would be no problems? That was unrealistic. The problems hadn't disappeared, but now I could handle them differently. That was the challenge. That made all the difference in the world. Once I stopped trying to change the circumstances, everything got better. I became happier. The event was a wonderful success."

Happiness depends not on what happens, but on how we handle what happens. Our happiness is determined by how we interpret, perceive, and integrate what happens into our state of mind. And how we perceive things is determined by our commitment. This is where balance comes in, learning our lessons and remembering the truth about each other. Are we committed to seeing the worst in people and situations, or the best? What we commit to, what we turn our attention to, grows. So the best or the worst grows within our interpretations, and within ourselves. If we see the past in a bad light, as lacking purpose or meaning, we plant the seeds that will grow into similar futures. This is why we refer to the past as our baggage—it's something heavy to carry around. By any name, it is that part of ourselves that continues to weigh us down and slows our progress toward happiness.

Happiness is our natural state, but we've forgotten how to be happy because we've gotten lost in our notions of what things should look like.

Think about the advice we've all heard: "Just *try* to be happy." The trying gets in the way of the feeling. We become happy gradually, not by simply learning some techniques or attending a "happiness creating" event. Happiness comes from experiencing moments of happiness—hopefully more and more of these. One day you'll realize that you had five minutes of happiness. Then, before you know it, you've had an hour of happiness, then an evening, and later a full day of happiness.

Making comparisons is probably the shortest route to unhappiness. We can never be happy if we compare ourselves to others. No matter who we are, what we have, or what we can do, we're always less than someone else in one way or another. The richest person in the world isn't the best looking; the best-looking person in the world doesn't have the biggest muscles; the one with the biggest muscles doesn't have the best spouse; the person with the best spouse doesn't have a Nobel prize; and on and on. With little effort, we can quickly compare ourselves into downright misery. We don't even need others for these self-destructive comparisons; comparing ourselves to our past or future can do the same thing. Happiness comes from seeing ourselves as being okay, just as we are, today, without comparison to others, without reference to the way we were or the way we fear we will be.

That "Why me?" feeling that comes from seeing ourselves as victims of circumstance keeps us stuck in unhappiness because it tells us to interpret everything bad as a personal affront. A sense of victimization comes from thinking that everything happens *to* us. There's loss and recovery, sunshine and rain—it is not personally against us. Even when someone hurts us, it's often not about us at all. Understanding this helps us move away from feeling victimized. Remember, your emotions and your reality are determined by your thoughts, not the other way around. You are *not* a victim of the world.

We live and travel in the Land of When, telling ourselves that we will be happy when certain things happen: when I start the new job, when I find the right mate, when the kids are grown. We're usually greatly disappointed to find that getting the things we were waiting for doesn't make us happy, so we choose a new set of "whens": when I get seniority, when we have our first child, when the kids get into good colleges. Getting our whens never pleases us for long. We must choose happiness over when. When is now. Happiness is just as possible with this set of circumstances as it is with the next.

Often we don't see a situation as it truly is. Instead, we focus on our image of what the situation "should" look like, or how it should be. By projecting our "shoulds" onto circumstances, we deny the truth. We see illusions. To see the truth is to know that no matter what may be happening, the universe is moving in the direction it is supposed to. That is why we can be in discourse, but our destiny is never off course. Whether the events in our own lives are the best or the worst, the world is set up to work, it is coded in a way that brings us to our lessons. It is designed to move us to joy, not away from it, even when we think things are going in the wrong direction. There is no problem or situation that God cannot deal with. The same is true for us.

Life makes us wrestle with all kinds of paradoxes. Thirty-one-year-old Mike was visiting his sixty-nine-year-old father, Howard, who was riddled with colon cancer. The doctors were not sure what the future held as the disease dragged on. Mike's visits were brief and infrequent. Although a loving man, he had a lot of issues with his father and was not fond of his stepmother of the past five years.

One day Mike arrived at his father's house after work, only to find that his father was not there. But his uncle Walter, Howard's brother, was. "Come on and wait," Walter said. "He'll be home from the doctor soon."

Sitting in the living room of his father's house, Mike fidgeted and kept checking his watch. Five minutes passed, ten minutes, twenty. Finally, he called a friend to say, "I'm giving my father ten more minutes, then I'll leave a note. I did my part, I visited. It's not my fault he's not here."

Uncle Walter, who had been in the kitchen eating, couldn't help overhearing the call. He apologized to his nephew for listening, then asked if Mike wanted some unsolicited advice.

"Sure," said Mike. "Why not."

"My father—your grandfather—died when I was in my thirties. Right about your age. I am now seventy-seven years old, so it's been over forty years since he died. The truth is, he was a jerk. I had mixed feelings about him after he died. Now I look back and realize one of life's paradoxes: life is long but time is short. After he was dead for ten, twenty, thirty years, I began to realize how little time I actually had with my father and wished I'd had more. I didn't understand that my life was long but his time was short.

"I know how you feel about your dad. He's my brother, I know he's not the easiest person to get along with. Neither

193

is your stepmother. I know you may or may not be able to work out your issues with him. But just realize that you feel there is time for them to be ironed out, because you will be around a long time. Your dad has cancer, and he is not."

Mike heard this in a way that sobered him up. He realized he could keep his anger at his father for the next fifty years, but he could not have his dad for that long. He decided to spend more time with his dad—not necessarily to work things out perfectly, just to take advantage of this time.

We think we will be happy when we get rid of problems or get past life's uncomfortable times. We want to live our lives in balance, but what we think of as balance is not balance at all. In fact, it's is very much out of balance. There is no good without bad, no light with dark, no day without night, no dawn without dusk, no perfection without imperfection. And we live in the midst of these opposites, these contradictions, these paradoxes.

We are a mass of contradictions. Always trying to be more, yet trying to accept and love ourselves just as we are. Trying to accept the reality of the human experience while knowing that we are also spiritual beings. We suffer, yet we can rise above our suffering. We experience loss, yet we feel love forever. We take life for granted, yet we know it does not last. We live in a world filled with less and more, with cycles of scarcity and abundance, big and small. If we can recognize these oppositions, we will be happier. Our part of this universe is always in balance, it just may not seem so to us.

Part of dealing with this balance means understanding that life does not revolve around our big moments: the promotion, the wedding, the retirement, and the cure. Life also occurs between the big moments. Much of what we need to learn is found in the small moments of life.

❖EKR

Most of my time is filled with just existing. If this is going to be it, I hope I die soon. As I mentioned, I often feel like a plane stuck on a runway. I would rather either go back to the gate, meaning get better, or finally take off. If I had my choice, I would live, but that would mean walking again, being able to work in my garden—being able to do the things I love doing. If I'm going to be alive, I want to live.

I am just existing now, not living. But even in just existing, there are small moments of happiness. I'm happy when my children come to visit, and especially happy when I can play with my new granddaughter, Sylvia. And Anna, the woman who cares for me now, also makes me happy, she makes me laugh. These small moments make just existing bearable.

❖ ❖ ❖

❖DK

An undeniably big moment in history occurred when Jonas Salk discovered the vaccine for polio in the 1950s. He was asked if he was going to patent his cure. Doing so would have made him one of the richest men on earth. He replied, "Sunshine is not mine to patent, and neither is this."

Most would think, "Oh, what a great sacrifice, what a big moment. That is what we wait for in life. If only I had a moment like that, a chance to be so noble and wise, I would be in the midst of real life, true life, important life. I would be so powerful and happy."

We tend to wait for those big moments to really "live life." But I sat on a panel with Dr. Salk in the 1980s, and as we worked our way through small decisions, I watched how he brought great love, great importance, great care, great power, to even the smallest of circumstances. In the smallest aspects of life, he found the largest. In the ordinary, he found the special.

✤ ✤ ✤

One of the greatest paradoxes we wrestle with is our own dark or shadow sides. We often try to get rid of them, but the belief that we can banish our "dark sides" is unrealistic and inauthentic. We need to find a balance between our own opposing forces. The balancing act is difficult, but a part of life. If we can see this as an experience as natural as night following day, we will find more contentment than if we try to pretend that night will never come. Life has storms. Storms always pass. Just as there has never been a day that did not give way to night or a storm that lasted forever, we move back and forth on this pendulum of life. We experience the good and the bad, the day and the night, the yin and the yang. We often teach just what we need to learn.

We live in these paradoxes, the many pushes and pulls. While it is true that our happiness does not depend on the external circumstances, we balance that truth with the reality of this world. We *are* affected by what happens around us. It would be unrealistic to say to someone experiencing tragedy, "This shouldn't have any effect on you." It will take a toll. At the same time, when we are at our worst, we sometimes find our best. We *do* overcome tragedies, we *do* go on to find happiness. The sun *does* break through the darkness. And in the midst of death, we sometimes find life.

We must do some learning in finding happiness—and some unlearning. We must train our minds to think in ways that are 180 degrees different from the ways the world has taught us. We must unlearn the negative ways of thinking. We must practice unlearning. By practice I don't mean practice being happy while walking in nature on a pleasantly cool, clear day. Practice being happy all the time, especially the next time circumstances are not terribly conducive to joy. Next time someone upsets you, practice happiness. Remain in the moment with them, hear what they are saying, see if it contains valuable information. But practice not letting it interfere with your state of mind.

Look at your patterns. Ask yourself which behaviors bring you to happiness, which deliver you to despair. Make changes, internally and externally. Does feeling jealous bring you happiness? Does yelling at someone or really zinging him make you feel good for long? When you are thankful, how do you feel? When you perform a kind gesture for someone, do you feel happy?

If you find yourself in traffic, rather than cursing, look around and see that everyone is in the same boat. Think about how others feel. Practice being kind to others. For those who want to take the advanced course, practice kindness anonymously. Do something caring or compassionate for someone without ever telling anyone.

❖DK

On a trip to Egypt I found myself sitting outside an ancient temple dedicated to healing. When I realized I had an hour before meeting a friend, I was annoyed. With nowhere to go I sat in front of this temple and watched the people who came to visit. I began looking at their faces, watching as they read a sign that described the temple and its healing powers. I wondered what healings these people might ask for. I then thought. "What if, rather than being unhappy about this stray hour, I pray for each one as he or she enters?" And so I prayed, guessing at what I thought these people might ask for in a healing. I prayed for them to remember their wholeness, their strength, their innate beauty, and their uniqueness, their love, their wisdom. I prayed for the healing of the past, and for the hope and opening of their future. I realized that I wanted a healing for the same things in myself. The next thing I knew, my friend walked up. The hour had magically passed and I was struck by my own sense of wonder and the happiness I was feeling.

We all find happiness in different ways, and from different lessons. Life's answers are usually simple. A kind woman in her mideighties named Patricia said it best. She seemed content with life, she was the epitome of happiness. One day someone asked her, "Are you as happy as you appear?"

She smiled and said, "I have had a good life; that makes me happy. I learned years ago to choose the things in life that I can feel good about and that will last. I know that sounds simple, but that's how life is. So many situations present themselves. If I had experienced them before, I would remember how I felt about them afterward, either good about it or bad. I learned to choose the good. If I hadn't experienced a situation before, I would imagine how I would feel later after making a choice. So many times when I was unhappy, I realized I was about to make a choice that would make me feel worse afterward. I just finally learned to choose the one that made me feel good about life. Choose the ones that make you feel good about who you are, that make others feel good, that you can be proud of and that will last. Then you have chosen love, life, and happiness. It is just that simple."

FINAL LESSON

Not too long ago, we were talking with an old friend. To our astonishment, this successful and beautiful forty-three-year-old physician complained of being unhappy.

She shared with us that she did not like her job, which really surprised us. We knew that she was a successful physician and professor of medicine at a major university—still she wanted more. "But you've got a great career," we noted. "Is there something wrong?"

"I don't feel happy professionally."

When she told us she didn't feel she was contributing enough to society, we asked, "Don't you still spend every Friday volunteering at the free clinic? Don't you still lecture and teach for free whenever you can? You donate to quite a few charities, too, right?

"Yes," she replied. "But it's not enough."

When she started talking about getting plastic surgery, we were floored. "A simple face-lift," she said, "a chin implant and a little collagen."

There's nothing wrong with plastic surgery, but we were sitting with a beautiful woman who did not need any help and seemed to be aging without so much as a wrinkle.

Finally, she asked us for our opinion. We looked at each

other, wondering who had taught our friend this nonsense. This woman—happily married, smart, successful, beautiful, wealthy, highly respected—had an embarrassment of riches, yet she felt as if she were underachieving, ungiving, and inferior looking. Perhaps she needed to work on her internals, rather than the externals. If she couldn't feel the success she had, how could she feel any more? If she didn't appreciate her beauty now, why would she feel different after plastic surgery? If she didn't feel good about the gifts she was giving, would donating more time and money make a difference to her? Working on the externals wasn't helping: she needed to realize just how wonderful and giving she already was.

Like this woman, most people today have been given everything they need to make their life work. Not everyone is as accomplished and as beautiful as she is. She is a good example only because she is such an obvious one. Most people have all they need to be happy—but are not. We're not happy with what we have accomplished, big or small. We are not content with our looks. But the truth is, we are never as unattractive as we feel. It's our inner experiences that are lacking. We have been given all we need to have a fulfilling, meaningful, and happy experience of life. We just don't recognize our own gifts, or goodness.

In counseling, people often discount or deny their goodness. Some of the most committed, giving, and loving people seem unaware of the impact they have on the world. From presidents of charities to the clergy, to those who work tirelessly to prevent intolerance, they seem painfully unaware of their goodness. They seem to lack the ability to see the truth about who they really are.

We often share this story with these individuals: There once was a man with a pure heart who performed good deeds. He also made mistakes, but that didn't matter, not only because he did so many wonderful things, but because he learned from his errors. Unfortunately, he was so aware of his good deeds that he became full of himself.

God realized that a good person who made mistakes but continued evolving would be okay, but one who became prideful would never find happiness. So He took away this man's ability to see his good deeds, saving that knowledge until his mortal work was done. The man continued doing good deeds, and all those around him appreciated them, but he himself never felt them or understood how much good he was doing. Finally, at the end of his life, God showed him all the good deeds he had done.

Often, we don't recognize our goodness until the end of life. We need to remember that we are here to try to remember our goodness and remind each other of our preciousness, and the miracle of each other.

From the beginning to the end, life is a school, complete with individualized tests and challenges. When we've learned all we can possibly learn, and when we have taught all we can possibly teach, we return home.

It's sometimes hard to see what the lessons are. It's difficult to understand, for example, that children who die at age two may have come here to teach their parents about compassion and love. Not only may we have difficulty understanding what is being taught, we may never know which lessons we're supposed to master. It would be impossible to master them all perfectly, and there are undoubtedly some dragons we're not supposed to slay this lifetime. Sometimes *not* slaying them is the lesson. It's easy to look at someone and say, "Oh, it's so sad, he didn't get the lesson of forgiveness before he died." But maybe he still

learned what he was supposed to. Or perhaps he was presented with opportunities to learn, but chose not to. And
who knows? Maybe *he* wasn't supposed to get the lesson
by forgiving. Perhaps *you* were offered an opportunity to
get the lesson of forgiveness by watching him. While we all
learn, we also all teach.

When people are buffeted by seemingly endless windstorms and their lives look like calamities, they may wonder why they have been given so many tests, and why God
appears to be so merciless. Going through hardship is like
being a rock in a tumbler. You're tossed to and fro and get
bruised, but you come out more polished and valuable than
ever. You are now prepared for even bigger lessons, bigger
challenges, and a bigger life. All the nightmares are turned
into blessings that become part of living. If we had shielded
the Grand Canyon from the windstorms that created it, we
would not see the beauty of its carvings. That may be why
so many patients have told us that if they could magically go
back to the point right before they got their cancer or other
life-challenging disease, and erase what was to come, they
would not.

In so many ways, loss shows us what is precious, while
love teaches us who we are. Relationships remind us of
ourselves and provide wondrous opportunities for growth.
Fear, anger, guilt, patience, and even time become our
greatest teachers. Even in our darkest hours we are growing. It's important that you know who you are in this lifetime. In our growth even our greatest fear, death, becomes
less and less. Think about what Michelangelo pointed out:
"If life was found to be agreeable, then so should death be. It
comes from the hand of the same master." In other words,
the same hand that gives us life, happiness, love, and more

isn't going to make death a horrible experience. As someone once said, endings are just beginnings backwards.

In the beginning of this book, Michelangelo told us that the beautiful sculptures he created were already there, inside the stones. He simply removed the excess to reveal the precious essence that had always been there. You do the same thing as you learn lessons in life: you chip away the excess to reveal the *wonder-ful* you inside.

Some of our greatest gifts from God may be answered prayers, but for all we know the unanswered ones may also contain gifts. In exploring the lessons from the edge of life, we become more comfortable with the knowledge that life ends one day. We also become more aware of life happening now. As we wrote this book, we ourselves continued to learn these lessons. No one has internalized them all; if we had, we would no longer be here. As we all still teach, we all still learn.

It's hard to deal with death before we have to, but it is at the very essence of life. We've asked the dying to be our teachers because we can't experiment with death or experience it ahead of time. We must rely on those who have faced life-challenging illnesses to be our instructors.

People make enormous changes at the very end of their lives. We wrote this book to take the lessons from the edge of life and give them to people who still have lots of time to make changes and to enjoy the results.

One of the most surprising lessons our teachers offer is that life doesn't end with the diagnosis of a life-challenging illness—that's when it truly begins. It begins at this point because when you acknowledge the reality of your death, you also have to acknowledge the reality of your life. You realize that you are still alive, that you have to live your life now, and that you only have this life now. The primary lesson the dying teach us is to live every day to its fullest.

When was the last time you really looked at the sea? Or smelled the morning? Touched a baby's hair? Really tasted and enjoyed food? Walked barefoot in the grass? Looked into the blue sky? These are all experiences that, for all we know, we may never get again. It's always eye-opening to hear the dying say that they just want to see the stars one more time, or to gaze out on the ocean. Many of us live near the ocean but never take the time to look at it. We all live under the stars, but do we look up at the sky? Do we really touch and taste life, do we see and feel the extraordinary, especially in the ordinary?

There is a saying that every time a baby is born, God has decided that the world will continue. In the same way, every day you wake up, you've been given another day of life to experience. When was the last time you fully experienced that day?

You don't get another life like this one. You will never again play this role and experience this life as it's been given to you. You will never again experience the world as in this life, in this set of circumstances in quite this way, with these parents, children, and families. You will never have quite this set of friends again. You will never experience the earth with all its wonders in this time again. Don't wait for one last look at the ocean, the sky, the stars, or a loved one. Go look now.

Life Lessons
Elisabeth Kübler-Ross, M.D., and David Kessler

About This Guide

2014 is the tenth anniversary of Elisabeth Kübler-Ross's death, but her work continues to be incredibly helpful and comforting to so many people. *Life Lessons* is the product of two well-known experts on loss, Elisabeth Kübler-Ross and David Kessler. It was their desire to take all the lessons they learned about life from the dying and those at the edge of life and pass them on to those of us who are still in the middle of our lives. The book focuses on fourteen lessons that the dying teach the living in order to live a better life: authenticity, love, relationships, loss, power, guilt, time, fear, anger, play, patience, surrender, forgiveness, and happiness. This reading group guide includes questions to enhance your discussion of *Life Lessons*, as well as insights from Kübler-Ross's and Kessler's work and suggestions for living a happier life.

Topics and Questions for Discussion

1. In *Life Lessons*, one woman, Stephanie, describes relaxing and surrendering to the moment when she realizes that her car is going to be struck and she might die. Before this

moment, she says she held on to life with "clenched fists" and that this was keeping her from truly enjoying living. What does Stephanie mean when she describes holding on to life with clenched fists? How might this have kept her from enjoying life?

2. In *Life Lessons,* Kübler-Ross and Kessler describe the lessons of authenticity, love, relationships, loss, power, guilt, time, fear, anger, play, patience, surrender, forgiveness, and happiness. Is this a complete list? Are there any other lessons that should be added?

3. "Relationships offer us the biggest opportunities for learning lessons in life, for discovering who we are, what we fear, where our power comes from, and the meaning of true love" (p. 40). Which relationships teach the most? Have you learned from a parent, a spouse, or a child? Describe a moment when someone in your life helped you discover something about yourself.

4. Christopher Landon describes facing death after his father passed away and finding courage from it. He says, "I realized you never know when you're going to die, and that you should face every challenge with that understanding." What made Christopher react this way? Is this a common response?

5. Kübler-Ross writes that "each of us has a Gandhi and a Hitler in us. . . . The Gandhi refers to the best in us, the most compassionate in us, while the Hitler refers to the worst in us, our negatives and smallness. Our lessons in life involve working on our smallness, getting rid of our negativity and finding the best in ourselves and each other" (p. 15). Is there really a Gandhi and a Hitler in people? Does there tend to be more of one than the other?

6. Kessler writes about how sometimes it seems impossible

to forgive. He says that a Holocaust survivor can teach many lessons about tolerance, love, anger, and forgiveness (p. 183). Kübler-Ross did much writing on the subject of forgiveness, especially as it relates to Holocaust survivors, as well. Why is forgiveness so crucial?

Enhance Your Book Club:

1. In *Life Lessons*, David Kessler describes his time spent with Mother Teresa, when she told him that she felt her most important work was with the dying because "a life is an achievement and dying, the end of that achievement" (p. xviii). Mother Teresa was known for her compassion and resilience in responding to the needs of others, and she was an inspiration to many around the world. Consider reading and discussing a biography of Mother Teresa's life or a selection of her words or writings in addition to *Life Lessons*.
2. If you wish to fully appreciate life you may want to consider volunteering at a local hospital, nursing home, or hospice agency. If you are dealing with the loss of someone, you could join a grief workshop or bereavement group.
3. If you have experienced or are anticipating a loss, writing a letter or keeping a journal that allows you to express your fears, hopes, regrets, reactions, and memories can be a wonderful outlet. You may want to write a letter addressed to a loved one or a friend, or simply keep a journal in which you record your thoughts and feelings.

In *On Death and Dying* by Elisabeth Kübler-Ross, M.D., and *On Grief and Grieving* and *Life Lessons* by Kübler-Ross and David Kessler, the authors establish a framework for talking about and understanding common experiences associated with loss, whether it is one's own death, the death of a loved one, or a significant personal loss. They underscore that navigating grief and death are natural parts of life and that it's important to be kind to ourselves and to each other as we undergo these changes. The following are some thoughts and guidelines from these three classic works that may help you cope with loss in your own life.

Mortality

"I believe that we should make it a habit to think about death and dying occasionally, I hope before we encounter it in our own life. . . . It may be a blessing, therefore, to use the time of illness to think about death and dying in terms of ourselves." (*On Death and Dying,* pp. 27–28)

> Try to embrace dying and death as natural parts of life, so that you are better able to face them for others and for yourself when the time comes. If you can be open with someone in their final moments, think how much could be gained by both of you. Overcoming the instinct to shy away can bring great insight and comfort, lessening the need for fear.

Happiness

"Part of the work is accepting the belief that finding happiness is essentially our purpose of life. Many people recoil at such a thought, saying such an approach is self-centered and uncaring. Why do we resist the idea that the purpose of life is being happy?

We feel guilty being happy, wondering how we can strive to be happy when so many people are less fortunate than we are. Or as someone bluntly put it, 'Why should you be happy?'" (*Life Lessons*, pp. 188–89)

Is happiness as a goal selfish?

Do we deserve happiness and why?

Why is it hard to accept the belief that happiness is our purpose?

Handling an Illness or Loss as a Family

"We cannot help the terminally ill patient in a really meaningful way if we do not include his family." (*On Death and Dying*, p. 151)

Support is important. Family reactions play an important part in a patient's own reaction and subsequent outlook.

There are lessons the family can learn from the dying.

Families often focus on the saying the "right" thing; in reality it is our presence that makes the difference.

Get help. A supportive friend or professional who is not as personally affected can ease the strain of making decisions and being there for a loved one by adding perspective when emotions are running high.

Family members can find comfort in each other.

Grief

"There is no correct way or time to grieve." (*On Grief and Grieving,* p. xi)

Take your time, there is no finish line and no judge.

Be sure to allow yourself to move through all of the stages of grief, remembering that some may overlap and recur and all are a part of processing and learning.

New grief may call up memories of old grief; it is not uncommon to feel a past loss keenly when a new loss occurs, especially if you were not able to fully explore your feelings before.

Don't be afraid to feel your grief fully and know that your losses are important. Try not to make comparisons in which you diminish the significance of your feelings.

Think about telling your story—to a friend, family member, significant other, or counselor. This can help you make sense of everything that has happened and help you move forward.

Unfinished Business

"Unfinished business is the biggest problem in life. . . . the more lessons we learn, the more business we finish, and the more fully we live, really live life." (*Life Lessons,* p. xvi)

Kessler states, "Fear doesn't stop death, but stops life"— remember to live in the moment and not allow fear to stop you.

Play is as important for adults as it is for children. Take time to add play and joy to your life.

Find Support

"Grief shared is grief abated." (*On Grief and Grieving,* p. 63)

Whether it's a friend, family member, significant other, therapist, grief workshop, bereavement group, or pastor—find someone you can talk with.

RESOURCES

The Elisabeth Kübler-Ross Foundation: www.ekrfoundation
  .org
American Academy of Hospice and Palliative Medicine: www
  .aahpm.org
Center to Advance Palliative Care: www.capc.org
Dying Matters: www.dyingmatters.org
Family Caregiver Alliance: www.caregiver.org
Grief.com: www.grief.com
GriefShare: www.griefshare.org
National Association of Social Workers: www.helpstartshere
  .org
Navigating Grief: www.navigatinggrief.com
Open to Hope: www.opentohope.com
The Compassionate Friends: www.compassionatefriends.org
The Dougy Center: www.dougy.org
MISS Foundation: www.missfoundation.org